SMART GAMBLING ™

John Gollehon
The Confident Gambler ™

GOLLEHON BOOKS ™
GRAND RAPIDS, MICHIGAN

MANUFACTURED IN THE UNITED STATES OF AMERICA

Library of Congress Catalog Card Number 2005900137

ISBN 0-914839-77-2
(International Standard Book Number)

GOLLEHON BOOKS, SMART GAMBLING, and
THE CONFIDENT GAMBLER are exclusive trademarks of
Gollehon Press, Inc.

GOLLEHON BOOKS are published by: Gollehon Press, Inc.,
6157 28th St. SE, Grand Rapids, MI 49546.

GOLLEHON BOOKS are available in quantity purchases; contact
Special Sales. Gollehon does not accept unsolicited manuscripts. Brief
book proposals are reviewed.

Contents

Gaming Books Authored By John Gollehon

Casino Games
Commando Craps & Blackjack
Conquering Casino Craps
How To Win!
What Casinos Don't Want You To Know
Gambler's Edge
Texas Hold 'em Take The Money!
Casino Gambling

The All About Series:
All About Blackjack
All About Craps
All About Slots And Video Poker
All About Roulette
All About Baccarat
All About Sports Betting
All About Keno

The Fun Facts Series:
Casino Fun Facts
Las Vegas Fun Facts
The Ultimate Winner's Guide To Gambling

From The Author...

The decision to gamble is a personal one. It should take into account many things, not the least of which is your ability to wisely manage money. If you frequently overdraw your checking account, exceed your credit-card limits, or otherwise spend your money recklessly—buying on impulse, for example—suffice to say, gambling is a bad idea.

If you do decide to try your luck, promise yourself that you will stay within your means. Gambling can be fun. Don't let serious losses take your fun away.

John Gollehon

*To gamblers
who mean business!*

Chapter 1

Introduction

Among the three principal gaming endeavors that we want to concentrate on, poker, particularly Texas Hold 'em, hits me as the most likely to succeed for the astute, and *studious*, player. But I could probably make the same case for sports and horse handicappers, too. It's just that my own personal experiences—successful experiences—would tend to support poker.

Before we delve into the games of choice for the "smart" gambler, I want to put all the games into perspective. I think it's important for two reasons: First, the great majority of players in a casino are slot players, and—although discussions on playing them certainly don't belong in this book—I'm somewhat uncomfortable chastising players for doing what they enjoy. If slots are their speed, I'm certainly not going to be the one who tries to take their fun away.

There are many players who would never even consider walking into a poker room at a casino, let alone sitting down at a table and watching the other players drool over them. But they will most obligingly sit themselves down at a video poker machine and "play poker" without what they consider the "intimidation" of the live game.

Second, there are definitive things players can do *in the short term* to increase their staying power at these negative-expectation games, thereby increasing the likelihood of being "in action" when the gods of chance decide to be kind to them.

Find the guy who just hit a slot machine jackpot for a cool million, and tell him what kind of a sucker he is. Go ahead, tell him.

Anything can happen in the short term, and many exciting wins *are* going to happen. No question. But over the *long* term, a negative-expectation game is going to run dry, and that new well you're digging will eventually produce the same result. It's just a matter of time. Trust me.

That's why I've always preached to the casual gamblers the importance of conservation: keeping their play in the short term. Limited sessions. Frequent breaks. Whatever it takes to minimize their exposure.

The *Other* Games

Knowing that you picked up this book because you want that elusive edge that only a skill-game can give you, I'll limit our "perspective" discussion of the games that can't give you the win-frequency you're looking for.

Let's start at the bottom and work up.

Keno is the pre-eminent example of a negative-expectation game. The percentages are so steep that you would have to be the luckiest person on the face of this earth to catch a really big hit. And you would have to be the second luckiest person on the face of this earth to catch much of anything. Just maintaining a decent stake is next to impossible. The percentages eat away at your bankroll in record speed, in spite of the fact that the games are dreadfully slow. In fact, the slowness of the game is about all it has going for it! Oh, sure, there are huge payoffs to be won... that's the big attraction. But the game is for dreamers, not serious gamblers.

And then there's **baccarat.** The game, with all its splendor, simply does not fit our parameters, either. But it's not just because of negative percentages; in fact, the percentages are quite low. But not low enough. A secondary problem with this game is its high minimum-wager requirement. Smart gamblers trying to get the best at non-skill games must limit their options to those games that allow them to start out with modest bets. And you can't do that at the baccarat tables! The game's attraction is its high-stakes simplicity, which draws high rollers and famous faces like a Hollywood premiere. Let me put it this way: If you don't typically arrive at a casino in a limousine, this is not your game.

I've already told you that **slot machines** draw the most players, and, not surprisingly, account for the lion's share of a casino's profits. With reel-type machines, the most frequently played, the trend today is toward entertainment. Machines are themed on television programs, hit movies, famous entertainers, everything and anything that will make you sit down and forget that you are actually investing money in these things!

The casino's signature game is **roulette,** and it's a tough call to eliminate from the list of professional games. Surprised? Let me tell you why. Because there are players lurking in the casinos—few, but they are there—who can beat the wheel through incredible electronic wizardry. The high-tech scheme works as long as the participants don't get caught. Not exactly what you had in mind, right? And that's why it's not really "smart gambling."

Of course, we can't forget **craps,** the game that sports the only bet in the casino without a house edge. There are a lot of pluses to this roller-coaster ride, and I must admit that I play the game often—perhaps too often—but I'll save that confession for another book. I've seen staggering wins at the dice tables, and fortunes made within minutes! But no special discipline or money management technique will change the negative expectation into a positive one.

Craps is the classic example of finding short-term anomalies and cashing them in. That's the only way to play the game. If your timing is on target, the mission is to hit 'em hard and escape with your winnings. Easier said than done because most craps players have a bad habit of sticking around far too long, making far too many multiple bets. For them, the short term came and went.

So what's wrong with **blackjack,** you ask? Simply put, the game ain't what it used to be. The casinos have toughened the rules and, most notably, many have added a continuous card shuffler to their tables. If you plan on counting cards, you must avoid these shuffling machines. They mix *all* the cards, including those in play. So what's the point of counting? Obviously, there is none at all.

There are other shuffling machines that only shuffle a separate set of decks while leaving the set that's in play on the table intact. That's OK. But that's not what you are more likely to find.

Among these staple casino games, believe it or not, craps is probably the smartest choice because it offers a bet that is the only fair bet in the casino: the odds bet. You can make it on the pass line or on the come, but it tags along with another bet that does give the casino an edge, albeit a small one. Veteran dice players know what I'm talking about. If you want to play the game right, pick up a copy of *Conquering Casino Craps.* But remember, as fun as this game is, it ranks with all the other negative-expectation games, so your best chance to beat it is in the short term. Keep your wagers in check until you feel the heat.

The "games" that we'll concentrate on in *Smart Gambling* are not negative-expectation games. The house makes its cut by taking a percentage of wagers. Although that's a bit elementary, think of poker, sports betting, and horse racing as a contest against other players, not the house. That's why skill becomes the key ingredient in your battle plans. Skill battles skill.

I love it already.

If Dave Can Do It...

Dave Friedman moved to Las Vegas several years ago after quitting his job as a mid-level manager. My old golfing buddy wanted to see if his incredible skill in rating college football teams could turn into a means of making a living. He wanted to gamble legally; he wisely chose Vegas.

I know this guy inside and out. He's a research freak. Put him in a library, spread books all over the table in front of him, and he's in his element. The boon of the Internet has been a blessing for this guy. He navigates the net like Columbus sailed the ocean blue. But newspapers and magazines—sports magazines, of course—are still his bread-and-butter sources.

It's worth noting the way he watches a game. He doesn't do it like you and I do. He tapes every game he can and studies the plays as if he were one of the coaches of the teams. He has a remarkable sense about him of figuring out at exactly what level a team will play based on games earlier in the season or, to some extent, the past season. He thinks it's the Number One factor in sports handicapping: Ranking teams in terms of emotion, desire, and toughness. Not overall, of course, but specifically for the upcoming weekend. A team that crushes a tough opponent one week might be low on his list for the following week. And if you ask him why, he'll give you an hour's worth of reasons.

Anyhow. Let me cut to the chase. Dave has been in Vegas now for about three years. Here's his track record. The first year he was a little nervous, and a little too conservative. He made about $25,000 net of expenses. And, yes... he reported all of it as income. He treated his venture as a business, setting up a plush office in one of his bedrooms at home. His record-keeping would knock you over. He hired a bookkeeper to help keep him organized (his only shortfall)... keep the books, and pay the taxes.

The second year was better. He cleared about $75,000. The third year was the charm. Over a quarter-of-a-million dollars!

The Value Of "Alerts"

Whether at the poker tables, at the racetrack, or in the sportsbooks, I keep two sets of alerts that I always refer to. Safely tucked in my wallet, these alerts, or signals, or whatever you want to call them, are always on, always there to alert me to a situation that can either make me vulnerable or make me a winner. One set is basic to all forms of gambling; the other sets are unique to a particular game. We'll talk about them more as we progress through the book, but for now, start thinking about things you think belong on *your* list.

Let me tell you another story that will help you understand the importance of adding discipline and sound money management to your new basic list. If you want to keep that "positive expectation," you need your own sets of personal alerts to follow to the letter.

A good friend who joined me on many of my frequent jaunts to Las Vegas during football season had one very annoying habit. He would walk away from the cashier's window in the sportsbook with green stuff hanging out of his pockets and then, as if guided by some sinister force, would head straight to the nearest craps table. We were out there to bet football, not shoot craps. But this long-lost friend would take his winnings from a great Saturday college bonanza and chuck it all, or most of it, at a cold dice table. The look on his face as he headed to the table told the story. He had way too much time on his hands until the pros teed it up on Sunday. It was one of those "there's nothing to do, Daddy" looks that I remember to this day, and it reminded me to start this piece with *my* Number One Alert: **Keep your winnings. I work hard for mine; I let go of it hard, too.** Suffice it to say, my buddy rarely got to bet the pros. He had all of Sunday to watch his picks win... the picks he couldn't bet.

Managing Money

I suggest you top your basic alert list with the same one that's on top of mine. After all, the very idea of keeping your winnings—as obvious as that might sound— should be front and center on every gambler's agenda. Whenever you feel an unwarranted urge to spend a goodly portion of your winnings, you should hear the alert. Is it time to leave the tables, to walk away from the track? **An important part of managing your money is not only the way you win it, but the way you keep it!**

The way I manage my money is two-fold: First, I play off my bankroll in strict limits per game, session, or day, depending on whether I'm betting poker, horses, or sports. It's a basic tenet of money management called "budgeting." All players say they do it; most players don't.

Second, I keep my bankroll... and my winnings, separate. In many cases, particularly if there is considerable money at issue, I'll put my winnings in a safety-deposit box that most all casinos provide today. If I'm at a racetrack, I'll often ask that a big winning ticket is paid by check. For those of you who try to hide your winnings from the feds, you'll probably get a W2-G issued by the track, so what's the point? Besides, if you're going to hide your winnings, I'd rather see you hide it from crooks, or, for that matter, from yourself! Who could do the most damage to your winnings... you, crooks, or a good tax account? Think about it.

House Money

It's a term that can only get you into trouble. The phrase is part of an old cliché among gamblers that I'm sure you've heard: "I'm betting with house money." The expression sprang up in the sportsbooks many years ago before the term "house money" was inserted for "the bookie's money." In fact, sports bettors are still the biggest victim of this charade, but I hear it around the track and in the poker rooms, too. So listen up: **When the money's in your pocket, it's your money!**

What difference does it make how it got there? Are your winnings a different color than your original stake? Are you applying two different values to money? I think so. And I think that this kind of attitude can only lead to reckless, senseless losses. Remember, when the money's in your pocket, it's your money! If you think of it as house money, the house will eventually get it back.

It's just another example of thinking the way the casino wants you to think.

An Example Of "Game" Alerts

Let's use sports betting, and specifically football, as my example in putting a set of "game" alerts together. I'll give you my top six, not my whole list, because I want you to design your own. It's more fun, and more satisfying, if your own, customized set of alerts wins money for you.

1. Key game: If a team I like doesn't really need the win, I'll pass. Late season games are good examples. If a team has already won a playoff berth, it's likely that you'll see conservative plays designed to protect the players. You might even see the starting quarterback yanked in the second quarter. What's worse, you might not even know this is going to happen until it's too late.

There is usually a wide array of teams that are not running on a full tank. So it's not that hard to find a team that's all fueled up for an important win. A good match-up to look for, as you might have already gathered, is a team that needs a win against a team that doesn't. But lookout for a betting line that might be *out* of line.

2. Key players: As an example, I remember a pro game where a key player had a lackluster game just the week before. There were rumblings about an injured knee but nothing in the papers. I bet against them that next week, and, sure enough, this key receiver had another bad game, running the wrong routes, or simply lacking his typical speed. He just didn't have much enthusiasm for the game. It was an easy win.

The next week, this player was on the sidelines on crutches after an MRI had revealed torn cartilage in his left knee.

What's important in this example is that the alert came early. I sensed a problem one week and cashed it in the next.

3. Emotional desire: It's perhaps the biggest alert I'm looking for. To really gauge it, I might have to wait right up until game time. I want to know my team wants that win and will leave nothing on the field. The list of reasons would be endless. I'm sure you can sense an emotional desire as much as anyone. But here's the key: You're not looking for signs of emotion from a particular player, or what I would call a "spotty" showing of emotion. You're looking for signs that *the entire team* is on an emotional high. And where does that come from, you ask? Nine times out of ten the fire is set by the head coach.

I'll always remember a sports bettor who told me—jokingly, I think—that he only bets teams with coaches who deliver the best halftime speeches!

4. Only a strong play: I remember the day I watched my friend make a wager of $110* on a team that we both liked and had planned on betting. I asked him why $110; why not the $220, $330, $550, or whatever we would have risked for that particularly strong pick. He said he liked it, but only for $110.

My answer is one that I hope you remember as you make your picks. I said, "If you like it for $110, but don't like it enough for $220, then you don't like it enough to bet it at any amount!"

He went back up to the window and hit it for another $220, realizing that he did like it, but had made

---

*A bettor lays 11 to win 10 in point-spread games. So, $110 wins $100. You collect the $100 in winnings along with your original $110 bet, of course.

the mistake that rookies often make—not backing up a solid pick with a solid bet. The game was an easy 45 to 14 win, and we only had to lay 9 points.

If you like it solid, bet it solid! If you only like it for a token wager, then don't bet it at all!

5. Information overload: Sometimes I get conflicting information from credible sources. The more I study a particular game, the more concerned I become. If I have the slightest doubt, I see no reason to risk a bet on the game. The concept of reading statistics is to take as much of the gamble out of gambling as possible. It's true of sports and it's true of horse racing.

6. Upset Specials: My friend and I are both pretty good at picking strong underdogs, although most of our bets are on the favorites. Laying points, even lots of points, was never a problem for us. But *getting* points always made me work harder to be sure I wasn't trading useless points for inept performance.

Among all the intangibles I look for when I'm leaning toward an underdog, a line bias tops the list. Whether a "regional bias" (Southern California teams affecting the line in Vegas, or Northern California teams in Reno, as examples), or a "bandwagon bias," (an inflated spread to counter a trendy or sentimental favorite), the idea of getting plus-points* *and* a team in contention is hard to ignore.

On any given Sunday, right?

---

*An overlay. More points than warranted.

Chapter 2

Sports Betting

Nevada sportsbook operators will all confirm what I'm about to tell you: The era of professional sports bettors—and I mean *professional*—peaked in the 1980s. Today's players are not in the same number, and certainly not in the same league as those tenacious gamblers from years ago, who would commandeer a cashier's window on Sunday morning and tie it up for an hour while hundred-dollar bills went one way across the counter. I'm talking stuffed pockets. Sports-coat pockets, pants pockets, and that occasional suitcase. The guys I'm talking about, though, were called "pocket players." They played out of their pockets bulging with literally tens of thousands of dollars!

Understanding the genius of many of these great players should make the unique concept of this chapter much more meaningful and appreciative to you. The lessons you'll learn come from this era, from the top sports bettors I've ever known.

One particular bettor was such a remarkable picker (and that's another term we used for them in those days) that he would often move the betting line a solid point or two. His wagering also moved his personal financial statement upward and onward. The last year of his remarkable run, the year we became good friends, he amassed over three hundred and fifty thousand dollars in net winnings. Not bad for 1980 dollars! And "net winnings" means wins less losses, net before taxes. Oh yes, he paid his taxes because he treated his venture as a business. He not only had that uncanny ability to pick winners, he also had distinguished character.

After his years of beating up on sportsbooks, he started a tout sheet at a time when these things actually were reputable… at least some of them were. He had his "steam" games and his "locks" and his infamous "daily double" for pro football.

With a staff to promote his sheet, he eventually garnered a whopping 15,000 subscribers! During these remarkable years, his picks were so respected that they were mentioned during a pregame sports program on network television. Absolutely unheard of in those days.

So why did he publish a tout sheet when he could have just continued betting, keeping his picks to himself? Because he had all the money he could ever spend during his "retirement" years. But if I knew him as well as I thought, the main reason he did the sheet was to show everyone that he could still pick 'em!

Now, is this all bull, you ask? Do I know for a fact how good this guy really was? I sure do. He gave me his picks before anyone else would see them. What he gave me were gifts. His picks were just about as good as getting a peek at Monday's sports section on Sunday morning. In his final season, he ended up with a 78 percent win record! That's truly remarkable by today's standards. By *any* standards! And get this. He never lost a single "lock" game in the three years that he published his famous sheet. At three to four games a year, as many as 12 winners in a row hit the board. 12 and 0! I want to see someone try that today!

Before we get into his secrets of picking winners, I want to make sure that you fully understand the in's and out's of sports betting. So here's a cursory rundown of betting football, basketball, and baseball. Even if you think you don't need this refresher course, read it anyhow. I guarantee you, even if you're a seasoned bettor, you'll learn something new.

The Point-Spread

During football or basketball season, Nevada sportsbooks offer a "point-spread" to handicap the differences in scoring potential among teams. If, for example, Miami is playing Pittsburgh in a football game and you know that Miami is a much better team, you can expect to find out that Miami is indeed the favorite and will be "giving" a certain number of points to the underdog Steelers. It's no different from playing golf with a friend who is much better than you are. To make the contest a fair opportunity for you to win, your friend must spot you a certain number of strokes, depending on exactly how much better your friend really is.

If Miami is considered to be a touchdown better than Pittsburgh, then Miami can be said to be favored by 7 points. The point-spread is 7. And on the board, the number " –7" will be written beside Miami's team name, which is the Dolphins. Sportsbooks use only the team names, not the cities, when listing games.

If you bet this game and decide to take Miami, you must win by more than 7 points to collect on your bet. If Pittsburgh wins the game outright, or loses by 6 points or less, you've lost your bet. If the game ends up 21-14 Miami, there is no decision on the wager, and it is returned to you.

It can also be said that Miami is "minus 7," or that Pittsburgh is "plus 7." If the game ends up 14 to 10 with Miami winning, you lost your bet if you took Miami, because with the point-spread taken into account, Pittsburgh "covered the spread." Subtracting 7 points from Miami's score gives Pittsburgh the edge 10 to 7.

But don't think of the spread in exactly that way. More correctly, think that Miami *only won by 4*, and that wasn't enough to cover the spread of 7 points. Don't convert the spread into a different final score than it really was. The score was 14 to 10, and Miami didn't cover. That's the way to think it through. If Miami had scored *18* points to Pittsburgh's 10, then Miami would have indeed covered the spread and you would have won your bet, taking Miami −7.

Fortunately, this same rule of the point-spread also applies to basketball games. But unfortunately, it doesn't apply to baseball, as we'll learn later.

Football "Juice"

Like a casino operation, the sportsbook itself does not actually gamble, or at least would prefer not to. A casino offers gambling, but the gambling is done on the part of the players, not by the casino. Since all games have a particular house advantage, the more players play, the more the casino wins. Over a long term, the casino never loses.

The sportsbook operation is set up along these same lines, and with rare exception, never loses over the long term, either. It's a function of the quantity of bettors, the accuracy of the lines, and, of course, good management.

In order to establish a "house edge," the sportsbook requires that all wagers on football and basketball (all games based on a point-spread) are made at 11 to 10 odds. This means that all bets, whether for the favorite or the underdog, must be made "against the odds," in addition to against the point-spread. For example, if you want to bet $100, a winning selection will earn you $90.90 based on 11 to 10 odds. If you want to win $100, you must risk $110. **To**

avoid the confusing payoffs, always make your bets in consideration of the 11 to 10 odds, such as $55 to win $50, $11 to win $10, or $220 to win $200. Regardless of the size of your bet, always remember that you're betting against the odds, and against the point-spread.

To understand how the sportsbook makes money, let's reduce the sportsbook's action, in theory, to two players, each taking one side and laying $110. Now, the sportsbook is holding $220 (called the "handle"). Assuming the final score is not the exact point-spread, and that the betting line did not move, the sportsbook will pay one winner $100 and return the $110 wager. What the sportsbook has left is its profit of $10. As a percentage, its profit is 4.5 percent (10 divided by 220).

If the point-spread accurately splits the betting public, and the sportsbook indeed receives equal two-way action, it earns the "juice" (its profit) no matter which team wins.

Many new bettors, aware that they have to bet ten percent more than they can win, incorrectly assume that the percentage against them is ten percent. As you can see, the actual percentage must be based over the course of both probabilities: win or lose. Experienced players who know this still believe that the true percentage is five percent, but, of course, that number is wrong also, as we've just proven. We can assume their error is using $200 as the handle instead of the actual $220.

Since many new bettors are surprised that the juice is "only" 4.5 percent, let's prove it again a different way, the same way that most casino-game percentages are determined. At the roulette table, for example, if the correct odds are 37 to 1 for hitting any one number, yet the casino will only pay 35 to 1, simply divide the number of units the casino has "shorted" you (2) by the total of both numbers in the correct odds expression (38). Two divided by 38 is 5.26 percent, which is the percentage against you at roulette. Similarly, when betting football, you are "shorted" $\frac{1}{11}$ of your bet. Divided by the total of both numbers in the correct odds expression (the correct odds are obviously 1 to 1), yields the same 4.5 percent.

$$\frac{\frac{1}{11}}{2} \quad = \quad \frac{1}{11} \quad X \quad \frac{1}{2} \quad = \quad \frac{1}{22} \quad = \quad .045$$

Line Movements

Earlier, I mentioned that the sportsbook will earn its 4.5 percent juice only if the betting line (the point-spread) has not moved, and if an equal number of dollars are bet on both sides. If either criterion is not met (it rarely is), the sportsbook might win more, win less, or actually lose. In other words, the sportsbook is gambling. Of course, we would also have to assume that the final score did not rest exactly on the point-spread. Now, let's analyze each aspect of all this to see how any variations can affect the sportsbook's profits, and perhaps *your* profits, too.

If the opening line is not on-target, the sportsbook will not get equal two-way betting action, which, of course, is what it wants. If indeed the opening line was not perfectly suited for two-way equal action, the sportsbook's option is to adjust the line. If too much money is coming in on the favorite, it might make the spread a half-point or even one full point higher to discourage more betting on the favorite and increase the action on the underdog. Once the betting action begins to right itself, the sportsbook might again adjust the line by moving it back down, but only if the action warrants. Since sportsbooks accept wagers of $10,000 (or more) on regular-season football games, you can see that only a few bets, if all one-sided, can quickly make the line move. It's not unusual for a football line to move two points when the action gets heavy. In that case, a large line movement is not necessarily because the line was wrong at the outset, but could be caused by unusually heavy one-sided betting by only a handful of players.

Accordingly, you might find different lines by shopping the many sportsbooks available. **Shopping for the best line is critical to a successful bettor.** As I mentioned, differences of two points or more are not that unusual. The line movement might help the sportsbook by balancing the money on both sides, but it also might help *you* by giving you less points to lay on a favorite, or more points to take on the underdog, depending on which direction the line actually moves.

Although the sportsbook moves a betting line in its own best interests, sometimes it backfires, and ends up costing the sportsbook huge sums of cash. Here's how it can happen:

Let's say Dallas opens at –6 against Detroit. Early betting is brisk and most of it is on Dallas. To counter this one-sided action, the sportsbook decides to move the line all the way to –8. If you took Dallas at –6 before the line moved, and then took the underdog Lions at +8, what do you suppose would happen if the game ended up 28-21 Dallas? What happens is you win both bets! The book got "middled," as the term is called, but a more appropriate term for it is "killed!" That's the risk the sportsbook takes when line movements are significant.

Incidentally, the sportsbook is also vulnerable to losing one side and "pushing" on the other ("pushing" means a tie). That would be the case in our example if the final score was either a 6-point or 8-point win for Dallas. In this instance, the sportsbook is said to have been "sided."

If the betting line did not move, and the point-spread did not include a half-point, it's possible that the entire contest is a push. If the point-spread is 10, and the final score has the favorite winning by 10, the sportsbook has to return all the bets. No action, no profit.

A half-point in the betting line ensures that the game will not fall exactly on the spread. At this number, all bets will be either won or lost... no ties.

If indeed you lost the game by a half-point, you might as well have lost it by 20! A loss is a loss. And don't make excuses for your lousy luck by blaming it on the kicker who couldn't make a chip-shot field goal, or the quarterback who couldn't hit an open receiver in the end-zone to save it for you. **You'll win some games that you should have lost, and you'll lose some games that you should have won. Accept your losses as easily as you accept your wins.**

Sometimes two teams will be evenly matched. When this happens, the term *Pick*, *Pick 'Em*, or simply *PK* will be shown on the board in place of a point-spread number.

In the case of a pick 'em game, you will lay 11 to 10, as usual, on either team to win outright… no points either way. A tie game in this case is a push; your bet will be refunded.

But remember, the oddsmaker doesn't necessarily believe the teams are evenly matched in a pick 'em game, but that *the betting public believes* the teams are evenly matched. That's a big difference sometimes. What's really important in pick 'em contests, or any games with a point-spread for that matter, is whether or not you believe the line truly reflects the scoring potential of two opposing teams. If it doesn't, in your humble opinion, then you've found a game worth considering.

It should be pointed out that betting lines are not as stable as they were in the past. Line movements can be quite severe on Mondays when the lines are first posted during football season, and the avid bettor must be quick to find any mistake. Within hours, the sportsbook will know exactly how successful the line is, and *within minutes* will make any needed changes. Most often, the line will become rock-solid by midday, and continue through the week—numbers that remarkably, week after week, split the betting public right down the middle.

The Money-Line

Baseball betting is based on a "money-line," which is really a means of rating two opposing teams in terms of "odds." Unlike football or basketball, where teams are handicapped by a differential in scoring potential as we've just learned, baseball is handicapped on the basis of a team's likelihood of winning, not by how many runs, but just winning.

To make this point absolutely clear, think of football or basketball as being rated in terms of points—how many points is one team better than the other? But in baseball, think of the game as being measured solely by one team's chances of winning, regardless of the final score.

To do this effectively, odds are quoted on the favorite team, such as 7 to 5 odds. And here's just one area where the picture gets a little cloudy. Usually whenever odds are quoted, the first number in the odds expression is the number of times a win will *not* happen. The second number is the number of times it will. The total of both numbers in the odds expression is the total number of theoretical contests it will take to develop a true relationship between winning and losing.

As an example, the odds are 37 to 1 at the roulette table of hitting any one number on the next spin. Since there are 38 compartments on the wheel where the ball might land, you can easily see why the odds are 37 to 1. You have only a one in 38 chance of winning. At the racetrack, if a horse goes off at 40 to 1, it will be lucky to get out of the starting gate.

These examples support the method of quoting odds in virtually all gambling events, the odds *of* winning. But in baseball, sometimes the odds are quoted *against* winning, and the first number in the odds expression may or may not represent the winning events.

So, in the case of our example earlier, where a team is favored by 7 to 5 odds, it means that the favorite should win 7 out of 12 times. The oddsmakers have determined that 12 games are enough to accurately rate the two teams. Seven times the favorite will probably win, and five times will probably lose. Of course, we don't know which games will be winners or losers, or for that matter, if the odds will turn out anywhere near what the oddsmakers have predicted, but we can conclude that the favorite has a 58 percent chance of winning *in each game* of our theoretical set. Yes, some bettors prefer to reduce odds to percentages. In our example, $\frac{7}{12}$ is 58 percent (7 divided by 12).

Now, let's put names on our two teams and see if we can make any sense out of all this. Let's say the Mets are the favored team, and Boston is the underdog. It's the World Series, and the odds are being quoted on the opening game. The Mets are 7 to 5 favorites over the Sox.

The oddsmakers have also installed the Mets as an 11 to 5 favorite to win the entire Series. OK, that's easy enough, the Mets have a better than 2 to 1 chance of winning; so they say. If the Series were 16 games instead of the best of 7, the oddsmakers believe the Mets would win 11 times.

But at the beginning of the season, many months prior, these same oddsmakers made the Mets an 8 to 1 favorite to win the Series. Does this mean the Mets had an 8 out of 9 chance of winning? Of course not. The oddsmakers were quoting the odds *of* winning, not *against* winning. As a percentage, it's only 11 percent!

Later in the season, just before the league playoffs, newspapers were correctly quoting the Mets as a 5 to 8 favorite of winning the Series. After all, the Mets had the best record in baseball and looked invincible. Although the numbers look "turned around," the expression is correct and follows the same form as the 8 to 1 odds quoted at the beginning of the season. The difference is because the Mets *turned it around* and became the odds-on favorite to win it all.

Seven to 5, 8 to 1, 5 to 8, odds of winning, odds against... no wonder the average bettor is confused. If the oddsmakers followed the same odds formula throughout the season, then the Mets would be a 5 to 7 favorite over Boston in the opening Series game. But it's quoted as 7 to 5 as if we're asking, "What are the odds that the Mets won't win it?" Are you still with me?

Converting the odds to a money-line is no cinch either. Here's the way most beginners do it: **Let's consider the 7 to 5 odds as being $70 to $50. Now, let's double the numbers to $140 to $100, same relationship, same odds. Sportsbooks put up the**

**betting numbers on a basis of $100, or just "100."
If the Mets are indeed a 7 to 5 favorite, up goes
the number "140" beside their name on the board.
A minus sign is in front of the number to indicate
that they are the favorite.**

Now, if you're going to bet the Mets, assuming you
still want to, **you must give the sportsbook $140 to
win $100, or any other amount to be paid in that
same ratio. You can wager $70 to win $50, or even
$7 to win $5,** although that paltry amount might be
under the minimum it accepts. Seven dollars just
doesn't turn anyone on anymore, especially in Las
Vegas.

*The best way to convert the "–140" on the board is the
same way the sportsbooks themselves do it. Think of it as
$1.40 and figure that you can win $1 on every $1.40 you
risk.* Give the sportsbook $14; if the Mets win, you win
$10 (plus your original $14 is given back, of course).

If you like the underdog Sox, you would ideally like
to bet $1 to win $1.40 and that would make it a fair
proposition. Of course, the sportsbook wouldn't earn
any profit over the long term doing it that way, so it
adjusts the actual numbers so that it can make an
"honest living." The book will ask you to risk a little
more on the favorite and take a little less on the
underdog. This way, the poor guy who runs the place
can feed his kids.

Incidentally, if you get your preliminary numbers
out of the newspapers, chances are they'll be listed in a
very strange way such as 6½–7. To make any sense out
of these numbers, simply insert a "5" between them

and read it as 7 to 5 for the favorite and 6½ to 5 for the underdog. The second number, not the first, represents the favorite... apparently another scheme to confuse you.

Baseball "Juice"

The sportsbook has tailored the structure of the odds payouts so that it earns a profit over long-term action. If the betting line is –140 for the favorite, the underdog will go off at +130, not +140. **In baseball, the sportsbook breaks even when the favorite wins, and wins when the underdog wins.** But sometimes it doesn't all work out as it should on paper. Yes, a sportsbook from time to time does indeed take a financial risk. Live by the sword...

All baseball lines are not all the same. I'm not talking about the actual numbers, but the juice that's in the numbers. Sure, the numbers do vary, and that's important in terms of shopping for the best numbers. But the differences in the numbers also vary, specifically the difference between a favorite and underdog team. That difference, if you recall, is the sportsbook's profit. And it's worth shopping for also.

Let's say our line on the Mets/Red Sox game is –140 Mets, +130 Sox. This line is called a "dime line" in sportsbook parlance, meaning that the difference between what the favorite takes from you and what the underdog gives you is 10 cents. Remember to assess the line as –$1.40 and +$1.30 for simplicity's sake, and the 10 cents will become more evident.

Some sportsbooks might offer a 15-cent line or 20-cent line instead, and you can be assured it means more profit for the sportsbook and less for the players. In our example, to make the line 15 cents, the favorite Mets might be listed at −145 and the Sox at +130, or perhaps the extra juice will come from the underdog as −140 Mets and +125 Sox.

In order for the sportsbook to hold its percentages constant, more or less, the 10-cent betting line will become 20 cents when the favorite goes over −200 (becomes greater than a 2 to 1 favorite). In fact, the 10-cent line becomes a 15-cent line at −200 in order to prevent the sportsbook's profit from falling below one percent. The reason for this variation is not to confuse—nor to deceive—you, but simply to maintain a reasonable profit level for the sportsbook.

As you can appreciate, if the difference between the numbers remained the same, while the numbers themselves became larger, then the percentage of difference would become *smaller*. The adjustment in the line is merely to prevent this from happening.

But don't be so naive as to think that all sportsbooks follow this same schedule. It always pays to shop for the best numbers, and the best percentages.

Proving The Juice

LINE	ACTION
METS –140	BETTOR A LAYS THE ODDS AT $140
SOX +130	BETTOR B TAKES THE ODDS AT $100

SPORTSBOOK IS HOLDING $240,
IF UNDERDOG WINS, SPORTSBOOK NETS $10.
IF FAVORITE WINS, SPORTSBOOK BREAKS EVEN.

$$\frac{10}{240} = .04 \qquad \frac{.04}{2} = .02 = 2\% \text{ JUICE}$$

In determining the sportsbook's actual juice in baseball, we follow the same procedure as in football, except we must divide our number in half since the juice is only earned when the underdog wins. Over the long term, the underdog wins about half the time. In football, the juice is earned regardless of which side wins.

Baseball's juice computation reminds me of baccarat, where the "juice" is only applied to the banker-hand, *and only when it wins.* The hand is one of two nearly equal possibilities. Assuming the hand is bet about half the time, and indeed wins about half the time, we divide the juice of five percent by 4 (½ of ½), not 2, in order to approximate its actual cost to the player.

Baccarat belongs in the same breath with 10-cent baseball because it's the player's best game in the casino in terms of overall percentages. Similarly, a 10-cent baseball line is the bettor's best game in the sportsbook, in terms of minimizing juice.

The Money-Line Vs. The Point-Spread

Now we know that the sportsbook makes about 2.5 percent or less (two percent average) on a 10-cent baseball line. If the line is 20 cents, the sportsbook will make about 4.5 percent, or approximately the same as football and basketball. Yes, in terms of percentages, baseball's 10-cent line is more attractive than football or basketball, but doesn't get anywhere near the overall action, in spite of the percentages, and the length of the season, and the number of games.

Why not give baseball a point-spread you ask, as if to suggest that the sportsbooks must all be run by a bunch of morons. Well, it's been tried, but not successfully. And here's why:

First, baseball is a relatively low-scoring affair. It's difficult to pick a number that would equally divide the betting public. Second, there is more parity in baseball that would make point-spreads unattractive. Third, baseball has been based on odds, not points, since the days of Abner Doubleday. Sportsbooks that have tried a baseball point-spread are plainly going against the grain.

And it works the other way, too. Football and basketball would not be successfully wagered with a money-line. Unlike baseball, where most all teams have a reasonable chance of winning a particular contest, basketball and football games are full of blow-outs— weak teams going up against powerhouses, with virtually no chance of winning. Such mismatches are most evident in college football where scores of 56-0 are not uncommon. With a money-line, who would want to take the underdog regardless of the odds pay-out? Even at +1000, or some such unheard-of number, a team that could easily lose by 50+ points is not going to get my attention, or interest, or money! Even if the skies parted above South Bend, and Slippery Rock's players rode in on golden chariots... I'll still take Notre Dame!

But what if Slippery Rock got some points. Lots of points. Not odds. Points! Indeed, the point-spread can "even-up" virtually any two teams on the betting board.

Sometimes, however, the mismatches are so severe that the sportsbook doesn't want to offer it at any number. In such cases, the game goes off the board and only the teams slug it out. Today, it would be unusual to find a football or basketball point-spread on the board at 50 points or more, unless it's "circled."

A circled point-spread number means the sportsbook will take only limited action on that particular game. If there's any doubt about critical factors, such as a quarterback injury or bad weather, the betting limit might be greatly reduced. Similarly, if the game is a meaningless contest or if the teams are greatly mismatched, up goes the circle and down goes the bets. The sportsbook is simply protecting itself.

In some cases, the game might go off the board as indicated by an "X" in place of the point-spread, meaning that the game cannot be bet, at any amount. And here's another good reason for shopping. An "X" on the board in one sportsbook doesn't necessarily mean the game's off all over town, but that's probably what you'll find.

Your Ticket

Unlike an illegal bookmaker who usually takes a bettor's credit, Nevada sportsbooks require cash at the window. In some cases, credit can indeed be established at Nevada sportsbooks, but the stiff requirements, including minimum deposits and residency, usually preclude the small or out-of-town bettor from participating. In addition, there is some concern presently as to the merits and safeguards of the phone-account credit system.

In any event, assuming you're playing with cash, a receipt for your wager is a computer-printed "ticket." The ticket is more than a receipt, however. **If your ticket wins, or part of the ticket wins, it's almost as good as cash. Give your tickets the same respect.**

Once your ticket is printed, you'll have locked in the odds or point-spread, even if the numbers change after you leave the window. The exception is in baseball when an "action" ticket is played and the listed pitchers do not start.

If you're an out-of town player, most all sportsbooks will accept mail delivery of your ticket and will remit the winnings by return mail. But check it out first. For example, Harrah's in Reno clearly states on its tickets: "WAGERS HONORED FOR ONE YEAR. WAGERS WILL NOT BE PAID BY MAIL." Of course, not only are the rules different among casinos, they also change. The smart bettor must learn how to read "the fine print" and ask questions when in doubt.

Don't be surprised or upset if the ticket writer asks for your name and address if you bet a large sum of cash. Nevada regulation 6A requires that sportsbooks report large cash transactions to the Treasury Department. Most often, the sportsbook will try to keep track of large bets, even those under the $10,000 minimum amount for reporting, in case you have more than one ticket played within a 24-hour period.

The idea behind regulation 6A is to discourage the "laundering" of illegal cash in Nevada—creating legitimate income from illegal enterprises. Laundering, in its simplest form—changing little bills into big bills—is an easy task at the sportsbook windows. Everyone has to play by this rule, although no one likes it, especially the sportsbooks themselves because of all the extra paperwork involved.

Other Bets

All three sports that we are concerned with—football, baseball, and basketball—offer you a host of betting propositions other than simply picking against the money-line in baseball, or against the point-spread in football and basketball. **Pro bettors concentrate exclusively on simply picking the winning teams. For the most part, they leave the other bets to the suckers.** We're not going to dwell on these other bets because they really should not be recommended. But since they are a part of sports betting, this chapter would be incomplete without at least a cursory discussion.

TOTALS: Betting "the totals" is simply betting on the combined final score of both teams as being "over" or "under" a particular number. If you believe the game will be a low-scoring contest, you would logically bet "under." If, on the other hand, you think the offenses will generate a lot of points, you would bet "over" the totals number. If the total score lands exactly on the totals number, all bets, either over or under, are returned.

You should be made aware that the conditions on which a final score rests are very difficult to measure. Accordingly, some experienced bettors consider the totals as a frivolous wager and ignore that part of the betting line. The only possible exception is in professional basketball where the scoring potential of such few key players is more easily judged.

PARLAYS: If you want to show everyone in the sportsbook parlor that you're a rank amateur, walk up to the betting window and ask about making a parlay bet. But be careful. The ticket writer might try to sell you a bridge, or a deed to a lost gold mine.

A parlay is nothing more than combining two or more games (usually up to 10) on one bet, in the hope you'll win them all and... well, own your own gold mine. The payoff for picking 10 out of 10 winners is enticing. But like the million-dollar slot jackpots and the $100,000 prize in keno, you're bucking big odds against you.

A "realistic" parlay bet of two games should pay off at 3 to 1 odds. Picking two winners out of two is indeed 3 to 1 odds.

$$(2 \times 2) - 1 \text{ TO } 1$$

Your payoff on a two-game parlay, however, is 13 to 5, not the true 15 to 5 odds that you should be paid. The difference is juice, and plenty of it. How much? If the correct odds are 15 to 5 (3 to 1), yet you are only paid 13 to 5, you are shorted two units out of 20 (15 + 5).

$$\frac{2}{20} = .10 = 10\% \text{ JUICE!}$$

The odds against you climb even higher when you pick more games. Forget it!

Many sportsbooks associated with casino-hotels distribute "parlay cards" throughout the casino, much like keno tickets. The cards list a selection of upcoming games (usually football), and all you have to do is mark your picks—against the spread, of course—then sit back and watch your money disappear through the casino's "black hole." In most cases, ties lose. And if one game loses, the whole card is a loser. Such a deal!

The parlay card gimmick has been tried, or is being considered, by several states outside of Nevada as part of a legalized sports-betting program, similar to state lotteries. Delaware gave it a shot in 1976, but it lasted only a few weeks because of a lot of snags, not the least of which was an NFL lawsuit against Delaware for "contaminating the game of football." But that's another story. I'm biting my tongue to spare you my own personal convictions about such narrow-minded thinking on the part of team owners and league executives.

To sum up, avoid parlays not because you're "contaminating" a sport, but because you're contaminating your wallet!

TEASERS: Here's another bet that's similar to a parlay, but the sportsbook will let you add points to the point-spread (or subtract points) to make your picks stronger. What you are allowed to do is called "moving the line." The number of points you can move is usually 6 points in football and 4 points in basketball. If Dallas is favored over St. Louis by 10 points, you can take Dallas at –4 instead, or take St. Louis at +16! Sounds good, right?

Wrong! As you might expect by now, the payoffs are worse than the parlays. Instead of the true odds of 15 to 5, you might get 9 to 5. Juice? I'm not even going to figure it out. Yes, ties lose... and you'll lose your shirt, pants, socks and anything else of value if you're "teased" by these stupid bets.

ROUND ROBIN: Are you ready for this one? You can select up to four games, and parlay any two or any three, or go for all four winners. This reminds me of marking a "combination ticket" in the keno parlor. And that's where it belongs. If you win two out of three, you might get a 3 to 5 payoff. On $5 you get $3! Is this legal?!

HALFTIME BETS: You guessed it. At halftime, the sportsbook will put up some new numbers for the second half, as if the second half were an entirely new game. It's a great way for you to get your money back if the game isn't going exactly as you had planned. And it's a great way to lose twice the money you originally risked. The sportsbooks are playing on the gambler's greed—a way to get back earlier losses. These guys are always looking for ways to take your money.

The danger of halftime betting should be obvious to those of you who have watched at least one football game in your entire lifetime. Have you ever watched a team get blown out in the first half, then come back and win it in the stretch? It's all a function of the coaches' famous halftime speeches. With halftime bets, we are not only concerned with rating the teams and the players, but now we have to rate the coaches. Incidentally, never make halftime bets against Notre Dame. The coach has his own speech-writer.

HOME-RUNS: To make this bet work for you, consult an astrological chart or get out your old ouija-board. It's really that silly. Surprisingly, a few sportsbooks in Northern Nevada and very few in Las Vegas are offering the home-run bet, based on a money-line such as –190 Kansas City and +170 Baltimore. Yes, it's a 20-cent line and "KC" is expected to hit more out of the park than the Orioles. So far, no sportsbook that I know of has a line out on grand-slams.

The only saving grace for the sports bettor is that you only have to be embarrassed by it during baseball season.

FUTURE BETS: At the beginning of a season, any season, the sportsbooks will have all the teams listed on their boards with the corresponding odds of winning the pennant, the World Series, The Super Bowl, The NBA Championship, The NCAA, you name it. Technically, the baseball All-Star game is considered a "futures" bet because the line goes up early.

In some cases, you can really clean up on longshots. When the NCAA basketball odds go up on the board, look out for the "Cinderellas." If you follow college hoops, you know that invariably some unforeseen team makes it to the "Final Four." Nothing scares a sportsbook more than future bets, which is why the odds against you are so high.

Incidentally, future bets usually generate the greatest line movement, and provide you with a good reason to shop. But consider these bets only for fun; never for serious money.

Unraveling The Home-Field Advantage

Now that you know how to make your wagers, let's get back to the burning issue of making *winning* wagers!

My expert friend knew how to "unskew" stats that other players took at face value. Here's a good example: Home-Field Advantage. Everyone's heard of it, but I'm willing to bet that most bettors rarely know when it counts… and when it doesn't.

Let's say you've studied the home-field versus away-game records of a particular football team. Chances are, these stats are meaningless at best, and costly at worst. In order to glean any valuable information from such a report, you need to know the following:

1. Are the statistics based on wins and losses only or are they based on the point-spread? Obviously, you are only interested in a win/loss record against the spread.

2. Do the stats reflect only the current season? Old stats are old news. If the season is just underway, it's tough to put real values on such few statistics, so most top bettors simply use this time for gathering data, not for betting. Still, long-recognized home-field advantages for certain teams will often carry forward year after year.

3. Do the statistics differentiate among opposing teams with a sub .500 record or a winning record (in contention)? Both pro and college teams in contention tend to beat up on a cupcake at home and easily cover the spread. Tough matches, particularly rivalry games, are another story. In the heat of battle, the pros tend to forget where they're playing; the college teams, however, often need to hear encouragement from their fans.

4. How strong is a particular team's fan base? It's a key issue. Wouldn't you think that a packed house would mean more to a home team than a stadium full of empty seats? Some pro markets and a dozen or so college towns really support their teams. Who could argue the value of Green Bay and Philly fans, for example, or the Big House in Ann Arbor or the Horseshoe in Columbus? You need to keep abreast of the teams that garner strong fan support.

5. Are the statistics adjusted to reflect the health of key players? The loss of a key player on either team would certainly skew the results. A back-up quarterback, for example, would feel much more at ease at home than in a hostile environment. Doesn't that make sense? In fact, this critical issue weighs in heavily not just for rating a home-field advantage but for all statistics you're keeping.

6. What about weather? Although most teams play in domed stadiums, many do not. Wouldn't you think that a snowstorm, or even a light rain for that matter, would reduce scoring and create miscues? But there's more to it than just the physical impact of inclement weather. Some teams like to play in the cold while others can't wait to get on the plane for home. Top sports handicappers not only know a team's likely performance in poor weather conditions, but also monitor the weather reports for those particular venues.

7. Are games that are on prime-time national television noted? Believe it or not, this is a statistic that carries considerable weight in valuing the home field. Poor teams tend to play better under the lights in front of a national TV audience, especially at home, while good teams are often unimpressive. You see the evidence every season. A team with a poor record taking on the conference leader on Monday night beats them straight up. It surprises many, but it doesn't surprise the veteran pros. "Spotlight" games, as we used to call them, can be unpredictable. Sharp bettors often take a pass.

What we learned from analyzing "the home field advantage" goes against the grain of what most players believe. Why? Because most players don't decipher the statistics; they don't do their homework. So let me do it for you.

For the pros, the point-spread value of being the home team is usually minuscule, unless those other factors we just discussed, such as fan support, health of key players, and so on, play into the equation. Otherwise, there is generally no statistical significance as to where the game is played.

If you're considering a pro game, and you believe that the linemaker has bumped up the line by giving the underdog visiting team an additional three points* for only that reason, you should be immediately suspect of that "gift." Be sure there are no other factors to

---

*Linemakers usually assign an arbitrary three points as the home-field advantage.

account for it. (Linemakers would most likely include such other factors in the making of the line.) But if you think you've found a double-dip (a betting line that appears to have a factor applied twice), score one for yourself and go pick the plum.

In the case of college football, the point-spread value of being the home team is far more significant than for the pros, and can, on occasion, be worth more than the linemaker has assigned. Yes, another plum to look for. With all other factors accounted for in the making of a betting line, it can only be assumed that the added value of home-field advantage comes from the fact that the players are younger, generally less mature, and therefore more comfortable at home in front of their fans *and* friends.

Simply put, there's a world of difference in handicapping the pros and the kids at college. And it's not just the big games—those great "rivalry" games—that make the difference. There's an electricity in the air at a college game that we all have experienced. It's easy to sum up the significance for college games: There's no place like home.

Coming Off An Ugly Loss... Or A Big Win: A Dichotomy Of Consideration

Once again, there's a chasm of difference between the pros and the college kids when it comes to figuring out just exactly how well a team will play following a mistake-laden loss or following a huge win. And the significance—for the pros, at least—is dubious, at best. Yet, it's a key part of the rookie bettor's arsenal of weapons. The idea is to determine to what degree a loss stuck in the players' craws, or whether or not a win will charge up a team so that it plays its next game with added vigor. As you'll soon learn, there is value in all this, but only if other factors are mixed in.

For the pros, the differences in performance following a win or loss are not significant unless the loss was particularly ugly or the win was particularly tough. Pros, as you might expect, tend to want to rectify an ugly loss. After all, they *are* professionals. A tough win, however, might take its toll. And I don't mean in the sense of being worn out; I'm talking in terms of satisfaction. Coaches from both ranks tell their players to only savor a victory for a few days. (College players however, might stretch the satisfaction of a tough win into the next game.)

Remember, the pros go through the season knowing that a 9 and 7 record might make the playoffs. They know that losses are inevitable. They accept losses—a few, anyhow—as reality. Two losses in a row usually doesn't hurt a pro team's playoff chances. (But it can be devastating to a college team's chances for a decent bowl.)

It's just another reason why the pros are less predictable than the college teams. The pros haven't heard their college fight song in a while, and they've got their millions in the bank. Let's face it, no matter how hard you try, no matter how deeply you delve in, there's no certainty which team will show up. How a pro team played last week is important to know, but hear me out: You need to look at *all the games* in order to lend any semblance of predictability. Only the full season's slate can give you a pattern to look for: of improvement, of worsening, or of some hard-to-spot idiosyncrasy.

At the college level, as I've already alluded to in parentheses, it's a different matter entirely. Once again, emotions can carry a team to another victory or dump them in the john. A college team's reaction to a tough loss may be poles apart from the pro experience. Worse yet, a college team's reaction to a big win might set them up for a lackluster performance to come.

There is more predictability in the college ranks when weighing the most recent performance. But other factors play a role, factors that rarely impact at the professional level.

When a college team celebrates a tough win (particularly in a rivalry game), and the next game is away from home, look out! The term that defines this emotional quirk has been around for eons. It's called "letdown away," and it means exactly what you think.

Looking at the other scenario, an ugly loss, college teams are more likely to follow it up with a shaky performance. Top coaches blame it on "trying too hard." All too often, the end result is another loss, not because of a lacking of confidence or skill, but a lacking of emotional stability. The confidence and skill were there; they simply weren't fully used. Sportswriters call it an "emotional loss." Sports bettors call it a "plum."

It's important to note that either "unexpected" result—a letdown following a win, or a loss following a dismal performance—is not as common with teams that have superior coaching and exceptionally mature players at the key positions.

Applying Your Knowledge

Obviously, the important stats to consider are the most recent ones. Who cares how a particular team performed *last* year. Sometimes there's a smooth segue from season to season, but most often it's a little jumpy. Always go with current stats. Ignore old stats that mean nothing.

Let's say you're into the fourth game of the season. You have three games to consider in judging performance. It's not much, and, accordingly, most pro bettors will go easy on these early season games. But by the eighth game, you now have seven games to consider in putting a prediction together. Not surprisingly, the veteran pro will probably make a stronger wager. **The bets grow as the information grows, as the season progresses.**

I don't want this to sound as if picking sports is a "system." It's not. The important points I've made are the "alerts" I talked about in Chapter 1. If you skipped that Introduction, go back and read it now. I don't want to spend your time repeating myself.

"Alerts" provide an important "check and balance" to my picks, not only in sports but in horse racing, too. Smart picks are made through skill in deciphering statistics, reading newspaper accounts, and surfing the Internet for the most timely information. But, as my old friend hammered into my skull, the keys of picking successfully are checking and double checking. Not to mention following a strict list of disciplines that any good gambler must do.

Secrets Of Beating The Spread

1. Establish your own set of "alerts." Run your picks by each and every one of them.

2. Bet only your strongest picks. Never bet just for the sake of "being in action." On a typical weekend, you might be hard-pressed to find more than two or three games worth betting. But that's all you really need. Don't be surprised if a weekend comes along when the only smart thing to do is watch. A greedy player who routinely bets a shopping list of games has little chance.

3. Concentrate on a particular conference or division of teams. Why make it tough on yourself? Forget the notion that the more teams you consider, the more chances of winning. In reality, the more teams you consider, the more confused you become. I live in the Midwest so I concentrate on Big 10 college football. I'll keep an eye on other national football powers, but my bets on those teams are rare.

While we're on the subject, **bowl games can be a source of major income for serious bettors. Mismatches are commonplace, there are often "home-**

field" advantages that are overlooked, such as a Pac-10 team playing in the Rose Bowl (trust me, those fans will get a much bigger allotment of tickets), and upsets are ripe. Why? It's not unusual for "good" teams to play at "great" levels in a finale game.

4. Always look first at the favorite. Most seasoned bettors pick the favorite a surprising 70 percent of the time. The theory is that a betting line is usually short because most typical bettors fear giving up significant points. Yes, it's a built-in bias that you should always consider. If a match looks lopsided, never hesitate to give up a bunch of points.

5. Pay no attention to others. Broadcasters and sportswriters (those who should know) tend to go with the flow—the public opinion—which means the point-spread usually stumps them. **(Studies have shown that the point-spread often makes the typical bettor choose the wrong team by over-valuing the line. Amateur bettors love to take the points!)**

6. Never underestimate the power of your intuition. A bet from the gut beats a bet from the heart every time. Most players bet a team they *want* to win, or against a team they *want* to lose.

7. Look for the plums. Give most of your attention to college games and look for mismatches where the betting line falls short. Mismatches are rarely handicapped correctly. The weak spreads may be correct for what they are intended to do—split the betting public—but often do not fully reflect the scoring potential of a superior team over a lesser opponent.

Taking this into consideration, the weakest betting lines put up by Nevada sportsbooks are usually in this order, starting with the weakest:

Early Season College Basketball
Tournament College Basketball
College Football
Professional Basketball
College Football Bowl Games
Professional Baseball
Conference Season College Basketball
Professional Football
Professional Football Playoffs

And you probably spend most of your money knocking heads with pro football players. No wonder your wallet's a little thin.

8. Do it in Vegas. Sure, I could just as easily have said "Reno," or any other Nevada town with at least one sportsbook, but I wanted to give the Vegas marketing gurus a leg up on their next great slogan… after "What happens here, stays here" becomes as worn-out as your shoes once you discover that you can walk the town easier than you can drive it!

Years ago, I made many, many trips to Vegas during the football seasons, flying out there every other week. My friend and I would arrive late Friday, get down on college for Saturday and the pros on Sunday and Monday, get a look at the lines for the following weekend, and get down on those, too... then head for the airport late Monday (or would that be Tuesday morning?) and catch a red-eye home. We endured this ordeal for several reasons, not the least of which was having the luxury of shopping for lines. Two other good reasons come to mind: We knew we were making legal bets, and we knew we would get paid on winning tickets. Very, very important!

If you live in Nevada, or within driving distance, you have an advantage that beats the heck out of connecting with some guy's server in Aruba, or having to deal with "the local boys."

In case you didn't know, Nevada is the only state with legalized sports betting.

When I spoke of systems a few paragraphs back, I was reminded of a story about a sports bettor who tried every system ever concocted. It's one of my favorites. A great story to close this chapter. And it speaks volumes.

A Man's Best Friend

All the neighbors knew that Myron had a little gambling problem. He liked football. He liked to bet football. He liked to bet football, big. Big BIG! He couldn't wait for football. Ask Myron what his favorite season is and the answer would be in your face before you even finished the question. "Fall! I like the fall." But he would hedge his reasons, just in case his neighbors might think he was a chronic gambler, which they already did.

"I like to see the leaves turning… the pine trees, you know."

"Yeah, but Myron, pine leaves don't turn, really. I don't think they even have leaves. They have those long needles, you know."

"Yeah, well, I like 'em anyhow. They turn brown, those needles."

"Brown, yeah, when they're dead!"

"Whatever."

Myron's problem with football betting is not an unusual one. It's easy to get caught up in it. And darn tough to quit. But Myron's problem was bigger than that. Myron simply wasn't a very good picker. He just didn't spend enough time reading the sports pages, or even doing a little web-surfing, although he did watch a lot of ESPN. While his wife, bless her soul, watched old movies in the living room, Myron took control of the big-screen TV in the family room. Myron believed that these big TVs were made for sports. He couldn't understand why anyone would want to watch football on some dinky little television. *The wife can have that one*, he figured. *She can just move a little closer.* That's the way Myron reasoned. A bit selfishly.

But he wasn't that selfish. You see, Myron's dog liked to watch football, too. He'd get all excited when Myron got excited. And that dog, believe me, would watch that screen just as intently as Myron did. Now it wasn't that Myron didn't have a lot of friends, it's just that Myron preferred Butch, his dog, over just about anyone else when it came to watching a game.

"Did ya see that play, Butch?! Wow! What a hit!"

Butch never answered, never did answer. But he'd look at Myron and sort of nod. Maybe a little "ruff, ruff." It was the best he could do. Sometimes he'd jump up in Myron's chair and they'd just sit there together, watching Young hit Rice for another San Francisco touchdown. Butch, after all, was Myron's best friend. Anyone's best friend.

Myron had one other little problem I should mention. He liked systems. In fact, he created a lot of his own. He always believed in what he called his "Good Home" system. He would only bet good teams playing at home. When it worked, Myron was convinced he had discovered the secret to picking winners. But like all systems, it worked and it didn't work. And when it didn't, he'd concoct another. He'd look for a team that had just won a big game and had an away-game the next week. This system has a name, too. It's called "letdown away." The logic, if there is any to all this, is that a team becomes content with its big win and won't play hard the next week, especially if it's traveling. The longer the team has to travel, the better. That's what Myron thought. And guess what? It worked for a while, but it didn't work very long. Back to the ol' drawing board.

Myron starting looking for teams that had a big game coming up, and a cream-puff scheduled the week before. His theory was that the team would be looking ahead to the big game, and overlook David with the slingshot in his pocket. He didn't know it but this system, like his others, has been tried over eternity. But Myron refused to give up.

Finally, Myron came up with a "new" system that required him to bet only teams that were favored to win by ten or more points, playing a team that had lost its last game by ten or more points. He could usually find one or two such games each weekend, and, for a while, this new system looked pretty good. But, like the leaves fall in autumn, so did Myron's new system.

In frustration, Myron decided to begin keeping better records of his bets. He wanted to see if there were any indications hidden in the records as to why he was losing. Surprisingly, one startling statistic turned up, one that he was a little suspicious of in the first place. It seemed that Myron was winning a fair share of college football games on Saturday, but giving back his winnings on Sunday, knocking heads with the pros. What Myron apparently didn't know is something that sportsbooks have known for eons. Beating the football spread on Saturday college football is indeed easier than beating the pros on Sunday. And there are good reasons for this. For one, the pros are simply less predictable. After all, the teams are all made up of top players, standouts in college. It's not unusual for a pro team with a losing record to surprise a top team in the conference. It happens. It happens all the time.

For another, college schedules are set up with huge mismatches, particularly at the beginning of the season. Too often, the line that's established to equally divide the betting public doesn't accurately reflect the potential of the two teams. Usually, the point-spread isn't high enough. Myron, unknowingly, may have been using this strategy while picking his strong favorites over weaker teams.

But Myron couldn't bear to watch all those great pro games on Sunday without a little wager. Too bad. Butch didn't care if he had a bet on a game or not, but Myron just didn't enjoy a game as much without a little action riding on it. Eventually, it led to his downfall. He wasn't betting to win, he was betting to enjoy. But just exactly how enjoyable is losing?

It got to the point where Myron's friends who took his bets wouldn't take them anymore. He had trouble paying off on Tuesdays, and he was getting pressure from his wife, bless her soul. He was looking for some-one, anyone, to take even a token wager, just so he could have some action. Any action at all.

One Sunday afternoon, with Butch sitting on his lap, Myron just sat there forlornly, hardly paying attention to the game, mumbling something about how boring the game was without a bet on it. Butch looked up at Myron; Myron looked down at Butch, and an idea was born. I don't know who got the idea first, but we'll give the credit to Myron. "How about it, little buddy, do you like Atlanta? I'll take the Giants. They're the favorite. You get ten points. Let's go ten bucks. OK?"

Well, Butch was excited. He knew something good was going to happen but he wasn't sure what it was. "Ruff, ruff!!" he exclaimed. Translation: Is there any food in this for me?

Atlanta won the game by two touchdowns and now Myron was having thoughts about stiffing his own dog. *What does he know. I'll give him a treat, take him for a walk, and he'll forget the whole thing.*

But Myron soon realized that he got what he wanted. He didn't win, but he was in action. Lovely action. So he set up an empty coffee can in the kitchen and wrote Butch's name on it. He started Butch's "trust" with a crisp ten-dollar bill.

As the season went on, Butch's coffee can got fatter and fatter. When Myron's wife found out about it, she decided she would honor that money as Butch's, bless her soul, and whenever she went grocery shopping, she'd take a ten or two out of the can and buy Butch a nice big Porterhouse steak. After all, it was his money. And if Butch could tell her what he wanted, it would definitely have something to do with food. A steak this week, a steak the next, and his favorite... steak, the week after that! It was getting to the point where Butch was eating better than Myron!

And Butch was fair about the whole thing. He'd let Myron's wife borrow a few bucks whenever she needed it. Butch, after all, had become a very successful handicapper. He had found the perfect system. The system that really works.

Myron picks, and Butch takes the other side.

Chapter 3

Texas Hold 'em

Texas Hold 'em is played as either a limit or no-limit game. Big tournaments and the games you see on television are no-limit, meaning that the betting limit for a player is the total amount of chips in front of that player. If a player bets all the chips by pushing them "all in," the player must win, or share, the pot in order to stay in the game.

But Texas Hold 'em is most often played as a limit game in casinos, poker rooms, and private games all over the world. The correct betting procedure in a limit game confuses many beginners, so allow me to explain it in simple terms.

Choosing The Right Betting Limits For "Limit" Hold 'em

Limit Hold 'em is played for different betting limits, easily confused by beginners who have played other casino games. A blackjack table with a $10 minimum and $2,000 maximum means that your bets can be anywhere from the low limit to the high limit. You can bet $437 if you want to. Any amount within this wide span will work. But at the Limit Hold 'em tables, what appears as a "range" of betting is really not that at all.

Typically, the smallest limit is called $2-$4 (referred to as 2-4), and represents the amounts to bet for the four different rounds of betting.

For the first two rounds, your bets must be $2. For the final two rounds, your bets must be $4. You can't bet less, but you can bet more by raising the bet. However, the raise must be the same structured amount.

If a player before you bet $2, and you want to stay in the game, you have to *call* that player's bet by also betting $2. Depending on the strength of your hand, you might want to *raise* $2 (for a total bet of $4), which means increasing the bet to $4 for the next player to call, if that player wants to stay in the game. The player who initially bet $2 will have to toss in another $2 (when it's that player's turn again) to continue playing.

If you don't at least call a bet, you must *fold* your hand, which means you're out of action until the next hand.

Technically, the term *limit* is misleading to beginners because the betting tiers are not really limits in the sense that you could bet less. You can't. And they are not really limits in the sense that you can't bet more. You can. Remember, your bets and raises must follow the structured nature of the game.

A typical poker room will have a wide variety of betting limits. Same tables; different betting limits.

Importance Of Playing Position

When you're assigned a seat at a table, there might be at least eight other players staring you down and sizing you up. In fact, most all Texas Hold 'em games are played full. The strategies that we'll talk about later in this book, strategies unlike any others you've read, are based on both a full complement of players and a "short" table with fewer players.

As you are about to see, Hold 'em is simple to play. But we have to be careful here. I'll always remember a phrase used in an old poker book of mine, published many years ago, that refers to this "simple" game as having a "veneer of simplicity" that serves only to dupe beginners into thinking it's not just simple to play, but simple to win. Indeed. We don't want the game's simplicity to make us put our guard down. As I said before, you must always know what (or whom) you're up against. Let's move on with that important understanding.

The casino provides a dealer who actually shuffles and deals the cards, verifies the bets,

settles disputes, and calls the winning hands. Since there is significant "position" advantage (and disadvantage) as to where you sit in relation to the dealer, each player takes a turn "acting" as the dealer. A dealer button, big enough that it's easy to spot by all players, rotates around the table in a clockwise direction. The actual dealer is responsible for moving this button to the next player following each hand.

Since the player with the dealer button is the last to play, that position and the second-to-last position are the best. The two players directly left of the player "on the button" are in a tough spot, especially for the first betting round. It's their job to get the engine started. Here's what I mean:

The Blinds

Before the dealing begins, both players directly left of the dealer button are required to make a forced bet. The first player to the left makes a bet called the "small blind." This term, incidentally, is now commonly used to refer to both the bet and the player making the bet.

The player to the left of the small blind has to make a forced bet, too. And that bet is called the "big blind." Most often, the amount of the big blind is equal to the smaller limit of the game.

In a $2-$4 game, the big blind would be two dollars. The small blind, incidentally, is usually one-half of the big blind... in this case, one dollar.

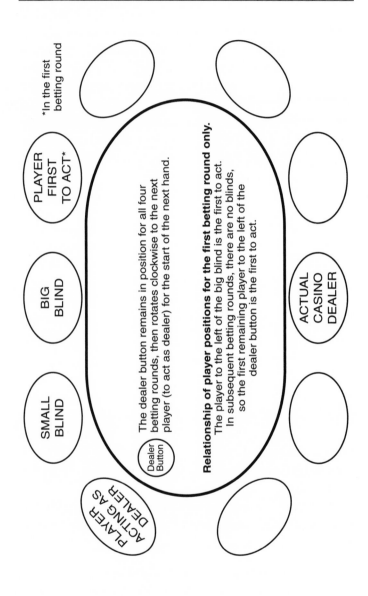

*In the first betting round

PLAYER FIRST TO ACT*

BIG BLIND

SMALL BLIND

PLAYER ACTING AS DEALER

Dealer Button

ACTUAL CASINO DEALER

The dealer button remains in position for all four betting rounds, then rotates clockwise to the next player (to act as dealer) for the start of the next hand.

Relationship of player positions for the first betting round only. The player to the left of the big blind is the first to act. In subsequent betting rounds, there are no blinds, so the first remaining player to the left of the dealer button is the first to act.

The blinds are like antes in the sense that they prime the pot and get the game going. In a $2-$4 game, the blinds are not really significant, but in a No Limit tournament game, the blinds are critical to survival. As the game progresses, the blinds grow by leaps and bounds. For someone who is ultra-conservative, playing only the best hands, the blinds will eventually eat them out of the game. That's why, in big tournament action, you'll often see pro players betting a hand that is not particularly strong. From the publishing vernacular, you bet or be damned.

The blinds are the answer to a common question from TV viewers who have been watching Hold 'em tournaments for some time and still can't figure out how the pot could be worth $60,000 when the first player to act is still sitting there, pondering if he or she wants to bet. Remember, the blinds are a real challenge in No Limit Hold 'em, but only of moderate concern in a low-stakes game.

The Deal

With both blinds posted, we're ready to play the game. The casino dealer delivers two cards face down to each player.

First, one card goes to each player, and then the second card is dealt to each player. Of course, you'll want to see what these cards are, so carefully slide the cards toward you and gently lift up the edges to read them.

Don't remove the cards from the table, for obvious reasons, and don't be so careless that other players could see your cards. The other important "don't" is not to put a permanent bend into the cards as you "peek."

If you think this advice is too elementary, I've got news for you. Recently, a big tournament was decided on a hand where the cards were inadvertently tipped toward another player. And there were only two players left in the match at the time. Guess which player won the tournament.

These first two cards are the only cards that will be dealt to you. They are commonly called "pocket" cards (or simply the "pocket"), or you can call them "hole" cards, if you like.

Whatever you call them, they are "for your eyes only."

Let The Game Begin

OK. We've got the blinds posted; the players all have their hole cards. We're ready to go. For the sake of discussion, let's say we're playing a $2-$4 game.

The player to the left of the big blind is first to act, and must decide whether to call the big blind ($2), raise, or fold. Let's say the player decides to just call. If so, two dollars is placed on the table in front of the player, not thrown into the pot. (When all betting for this first round is completed, the bets are moved into the pot.)

Now it's up to the next player, faced with the same decision: call the bet, raise, or fold. If this player elects to raise, $4 is pushed out on the table ($2 to call the bet and $2 to raise).

The next player goes through these same options, then the next, and the next, until the betting gets around to the small blind. If the small blind wants to stay in the pot, another three dollars needs to be wagered ($1 to match the big blind and $2 to call the raise). Remember the small blind is only in for a dollar; the big blind is in for *two* dollars. The big blind needs only to invest another $2 in the pot (matching the raise) in order to continue in the game.

The Flop

The second round of betting is where the game "get's good," as my poker buddy likes to say. In fact, it's where many hands are won or lost.

The dealer will "flop" (place) three cards in the center of the table face up. These cards are the first of five community cards that all players can use—along with their pocket cards—to make the best poker hand.

Before the flop, and the placing of the remaining two community cards "on the board" (the table) in later betting rounds, the dealer always burns a card, which means to take the top card out of play.

The betting begins with the first active player (a player still in the game) who is left of (and closest to) the player with the dealer button. There are no more blinds to contend with. And some players may have folded during the first round. That's why the first player to act could very well be the player who had to post the small blind in the first round. But if that player had folded, and if the next two players had folded also, then the next player (moving clockwise around the table) is the first to start the betting round.

I should note at this point that the first player to start the betting in this second round has an additional option available that wasn't available in the first round. Besides betting, this player could also "check." To "check" means to "pass."

To see if you're really following this, let me ask you a question. Why couldn't a player check in the first round?

Sure. You've got it. It's because the blinds made their forced bets and you can't check a bet; you can only call it or raise it… or fold.

The Turn Card

The third round of betting begins with the dealer placing a fourth card on the board directly beside the flop. This card, called the "turn" card, can greatly change the complexion of the remaining players' hands. Why? Because after the turn card has been seen, there is only one community card left to be placed. The third round is clearly a do-or-die decision for the remaining players.

Again, the third-round betting begins with the first active player (a player still in the game) who is left of (and closest to) the player with the dealer button.

Of great importance, the betting limit has doubled in this third round. The limit of two dollars for the first two rounds has been increased to four dollars for this third round and the final round to come. Is this something you should consider in the third round? No! It's something you should consider in the *second* round. An important aspect of poker is looking one jump ahead.

The River Card

The fourth and final round of betting starts with the dealer placing a fifth card directly beside the turn card. This card, called the "river," will pretty much tell you whether or not it's time to go for the jugular, or to limp out of the game.

And that's a rather accurate appraisal of your choices. You see, at this stage of the game, you're virtually assured of significant betting action that you must be prepared for. If your hand improved "on the river," that's great. You might want to stay in and fight for the pot. If not, and depending on the number of players left to fight with, you might need to turn your tail.

There is a showdown if more than one player remains after betting concludes. All active players turn over their pocket cards so that the dealer can confirm the winning hand.

If one player has bounced all the others out of the game, there is no showing of the cards (in fact, the winning player would be well-advised not to).

CARDS DEALT DURING THE 4 BETTING ROUNDS

ROUND	CARDS DEALT
1	2 (Pocket cards)
2	3 (the Flop)
3	1 (the Turn)
4	1 (the River)

The Fine Art Of Folding

This is as good a place as any to mention the psychological aspect of folding a hand, a critical part of any poker game that you need to deal with properly. Which means sensibly, rationally, and realistically.

Folding early on, say, during the first betting round, is tough to do for some players because… well, because they came to play. They don't want to just sit there watching other players play.

If you remember anything from this book, remember this: Folding is a common occurrence. At least it should be. More often than not, folding your hand is the right move. Need I remind you: **You're not there to play, you're there to win!**

Folding in the later rounds can be tough to do for some players, too. They've stuck around for most of the game, made an investment they hate to walk away from, and actually feel obligated to stay in the game, maybe with a so-so hand, maybe just hanging on with the hope of catching the right card.

Listen up: If your pocket cards weren't strong, and you did little to improve your hand to the end, you weren't staying in a game, you were staying on a sinking ship. Those who folded took the lifeboats. And you? You're going down with the ship.

Good poker players know not only to get out of a bad hand, but *when* to get out. And you know what? It doesn't take an Einstein to figure it out. Any player with common sense… and a good *intuitive* sense, can make these important stay-in/get-out decisions just as well as the pros can do.

Rank Of Hands

If it just so happens that you are not that familiar with the rank of poker hands, a listing follows in order of strength. You absolutely must know the ranking by heart. And it's not tough at all.

I can't forget a young player, many years ago, who stopped the table cold by asking: "I forgot, does a full house beat a flush?"

As a standard poker rule, the ace may count as either high or low in making a straight, A-2-3-4-5, or 10-J-Q-K-A. This rule reminds me of another recollection from my earlier days of poker. At the showdown, a player turned over his cards and announced that he had a straight. But the dealer told him he did not have a straight. "Sure I do," he said. "Seven, eight, nine, ten, and eleven." He had a 7-8-9-10-ace. That's right. This rookie poker player came over from the blackjack tables where an ace counts as one or eleven!

RANK OF POKER HANDS (IN DESCENDING VALUE)

HAND	DESCRIPTION
Royal Flush	Only the 10, jack, queen, king, and ace of the same suit.
Straight Flush	Any five cards in consecutive value, of the same suit, such as 2, 3, 4, 5, and 6 of diamonds.
Four-of-a-Kind	Any four cards of the same value (all four cards of the four different suits) such as the 8 of hearts, diamonds, spades, and clubs.
Full House	Five cards that include a pair and three-of-a-kind, such as a pair of kings and three 10s.
Flush	Any five cards of the same suit, such as 8, 10, jack, king, and ace of hearts.
Straight	Any five cards in consecutive value, not of the same suit, such as 4 of clubs, 5 of hearts, 6 and 7 of spades, and 8 of diamonds.
Three-of-a-Kind	Any three cards of the same value such as three queens.
Two Pair	Two pairs of different equal value cards such as two 3s and two 10s.
One Pair	Any two cards of the same value, such as two 3s
High Card	The highest card in your hand. (If no player has at least a pair, the high card wins.)

The Key Strategy:
Rank Of Pocket Cards

The key strategy of Hold 'em, whether a limit or no-limit game, is knowing which pocket cards are worth keeping. Remember, the pocket cards are the only hole cards you'll get. The community cards belong to *all* the players. Clearly, what makes your pocket cards strong are basically three factors:

1. The likelihood of getting beat with an overcard.* For example, a pair of 6s is not a strong hand because it's highly likely that another player, or players, have:

    (1) one card that's higher than a 6, or
    (2) *two* cards that are higher than a 6, or
    (3) a higher pair.

The only card on the board that could improve your hand is another 6. But if a player holds two higher cards of different value, *either* of those card values appearing on the board (an overcard) will beat you if you don't draw a 6. The only real hope you have is that other players do not pair up, or, if they do, they pair below your 6s. That's a lot to hope for.

2. The high value of your cards. Obviously, an ace is a good card to have in your pocket. If the other card is also high—say, a king, for example—that's even better. If the other card is also an ace, you've got the best possible hole cards.

But, if you stay in with a 5 and 6 off-suit, for example, these are certainly not high cards and are easily beat. Your only hope is to make two pair or get

---

*A community card higher in value than both of your hole cards.

real lucky and fill a straight. If the 5 and 6 are suited, that does change the complexion of your hand since a flush also becomes a possibility.

Take this to the bank: As much as luck does play a big part in this game, you never want to put yourself in a position where you are stretching it too far! You can stretch it once, maybe twice, but beyond that, Lady Luck will be stretching *you!*

3. The number of players in the game. As the number of active players decreases, you have fewer chances of getting beat by a lucky draw. You cannot merely assume that the remaining players all have strong hands. Regardless, the fewer the players, the fewer shots taken at you.

This is particularly important in games that are not full. If a table only sports four or five players, for example, the rank of pocket cards changes somewhat by the addition of lesser values to the list. You don't necessarily need the big guns to beat half an army.

BEST CARDS IN THE POCKET
(IN DESCENDING ORDER)

FULL TABLE	HALF TABLE (ADDITIONAL HANDS)
A-A	A-J
K-K	10-10
A-K	A-10
Q-Q	K-J
A-Q	K-10
J-J	Q-10
K-Q	J-10

Note: If the unpaired hands are suited, it's an obvious plus. Surprisingly, however, the rank does not change significantly whether suited or off-suit, in these higher-value cards.

Pocket card strategy is not the same as Basic Strategy at blackjack where a mathematically correct player action is called for by the appearance of three cards: the dealer up-card and a player's two cards. Blackjack strategy works because it is not subject to the actions of other players. But at the poker tables, the *way* other players play their hands does indeed affect the value of your pocket cards.

The three main factors we just covered are clearly most important. You must routinely look at each hand in terms of these factors in evaluating your hand. But if the way other players play their hands also affects your own hand evaluation, as we also just learned, then there must be more criteria to consider, and there is. Knowing all the factors, not just the top three, can separate winners from losers.

Pocket card evaluation is the real essence of the game, no question, but **the values you place on your hand are always relative to the conditions at a particular table at a particular time. Never think of pocket card values as absolutes.** For example, are you playing a limit or no-limit game? It makes a big difference!

Here are additional factors that you must weigh:

LIMIT GAME:

1. Are you playing in a low-limit or high-limit game? Remember, players in a low-limit game tend to play out their hands, so there is rarely any real playing strategy to contend with. The best hand wins. It's often

that simple. So the top hands (as listed under FULL TABLE) are what you want to see. Higher limit games, such as $10-$20, can be won or lost on sound betting strategies, even with weaker hands. The hands listed under HALF TABLE may be appropriately played, if you know how to hide the "weakness." **Make other players make mistakes… make them fold when they should stay, and stay when they should fold.** To do this, take control of the game. Most players don't raise as often as they should. Instead of calling, as you might often do, raise instead… and take control.

2. The quality of play is of significant importance to hand valuation in a limit game. Are you up against good players or beginners? Surprisingly, this is not usually a consideration in a no-limit game, particularly a high buy-in tournament, because you can fairly assume that all players are good. Maybe *too* good. My choice has always been a progression of limit games, starting with $5-$10, and moving up through $10-$20, and perhaps to $20-$40 if my success continues. The varying quality of players I run into along the way is quite remarkable. A key to winning—for me, at least—is how quickly I can discern the other players' abilities.

3. Many casinos and poker rooms now offer special promotions on their limit games, particularly the low-limit games. There are cash prizes for certain low hands that win the pot, and even for a low hand that draws out to make a good hand, win or lose. The minimum low hand and high hand to make is specified in the promotion's rules. These gimmicks should always be

avoided. Sure, there are times when the prize money is tempting, but I have yet to see a promotional offer that would justify such reckless play.

NO-LIMIT GAME:

1. Remember, the price of the blinds can have a dramatic impact on the hands you play. Until the blinds become significant, play in the same manner as you would a higher-priced limit game. For many players, that means a conservative approach, both in the hands they play and the way they play them. Such players are keyed to two things: staying in the game, and building up rations.

2. As the blinds increase, you'll reach the point where you will have to play weak hands to remain in the game. And it's always late in the game when the best players make their moves. **Clearly, the reason you see many of the same pros at numerous final tables is because they know how to play weak hands.** Skillful bluffs are the obvious edge, but getting a read on the other players is just as important.

It's interesting to note that many of the non-professionals who make it into the later rounds will often switch gears to an ultra-conservative strategy. Sensing that they are close to finishing "in the money," they tend to play as if they're in a cheap limit game, tossing away the best of the weak hands. With a dwindling stake, they've already committed themselves to 15th place and a small piece of the cash prize.

Not the attitude of a winner!

Tough Hands

In either a limit or no-limit game, don't play for just a flush. Some players would even say… "for just a straight." Most hands are won on high pairs or trips; you should always make this fact a key consideration.

All tough hands are not equal, although they may appear equally poor to the rank beginner. For example, 2-3 suited compared to 6-7 suited is weaker on two counts. For the obvious reason, the card values are smaller. For another, there is a better chance of making a straight with 6-7. Even though straights should be a secondary consideration, you must be able to clearly see how one hand is better than the other in making a straight. The weaker 2-3 will only team up with a 4-5-6 or A-4-5, whereas the 6-7 can team up with 3-4-5, 4-5-8, 5-8-9, or 8-9-10.

The hope, of course, is to have two high pocket cards, suited, such as K-Q, where either one or both can pair up with like-value cards on the board for a pair, two pair, three-of-a-kind, or a full house. But the extra value here is in making a *high* straight or a flush. Remember, though, you didn't keep this hand because it had flush draw possibilities or straight draw possibilities. You kept the hand because of the stronger possibilities of making a high pair or pairs, trips, or a full boat.

It's worth noting that many tough hands don't even give you the possibility of a straight draw. A hand of 4-10, for example, won't make it the easy way (using both pocket cards) because there's too big of a gap between the card values. The thin straight possibilities you have only allow you to use one of your pocket cards. You would need to get really lucky with, say, J-Q-K-A on the board! Fat chance!

With a hand like 4-10 off-suit, you can only hope to pair up, preferably with another 10, but a better "hope" is that the other players left in the game have hands just as shaky as yours!

There's no question about it. Being forced to play a bad, or even marginal, hand is the "gamble" of no-limit Hold 'em.

Neat Things To Know

• The distribution and dispersion of cards is called **permeation,** a term popular with blackjack before the age of continuous shuffling machines, and still somewhat of interest to baccarat players, but of greater interest now to poker players. Is there an anomaly in the mixing of cards? Is there a predictable element to the selection of community cards? If two aces are tossed into the pile together, might they stay together for the next deal?

This novel concept should not be taken lightly. Card values tend to "clump" through the shuffling process, particularly noticeable when a fresh deck is placed into service. Break the seal on a new deck and you'll see that the cards run in numerical order; the face cards, for example, are grouped together.

Test this theory yourself. Mix the cards exactly as a dealer does, and look for evidence of clumping as the cards are dealt, particularly the flop. Experts who study the randomness of selection (keno and lottery balls, and even roulette numbers, are key examples) believe that a perfectly random shuffle is all but impossible.

• Would you rather play at a table with players you know, or with players you've never seen before? It's an easy answer, but in that answer lies another important aspect of poker personality. You have no information to use about players whom you've never played against. And, if you sit at that table and never learn a damn thing about them, you might be in for a rough ride. Players who won't let other players penetrate their "shield," are ahead of the game.

Learn how to play and maintain a **mystique.** The idea is that you remain a mystery to the other players. Try to become an unpredictable, hard-to-read combatant; mix up your actions well enough that no one has an inkling whether you have rockets in your pocket or 10s that need a booster.

• Professional players frequently seen in televised tournaments always tape the program and study it over and over. Poker players who are really into physical analysis among players tend to perform better. Players I know who believe they have developed a new sense (would that be the sixth?) to add to their arsenal call it **"super-vision."** They scrutinize all the other players, of course… but they also scrutinize themselves.

It's why nervous, fidgety players rarely win the marbles. You can wear sunglasses or pull down the bill of your baseball cap, but you can't hide yourself! That's right. Most of the "information give-away" comes from subtle body movements. Your mystique is not only on the table, it's in your chair! Sit there like a rock!

• Blackjack and poker have an interesting similarity in the value of **small cards.** They're not worth much to a blackjack player; they're worth even less at a poker table. Go with large-value pocket cards and stick with this practice. Let other players play the small cards. (In no-limit games, sometimes you have to play hands that are not particularly strong because of the increasing blinds. But you can still be judicious about it.)

Most players overvalue **small pairs.** Any pair of 10s or smaller are ripe for getting eaten (by an overcard, of course). You're not playing a video poker machine. This is a live game. It's too easy to lose on your pair of 8s with a 9-or-better overcard on the board. Incidentally, poker room managers often refer to limit games as "live" or "structured" games, so don't let the terms confuse you.

• When you watch players in a televised tournament betting tens of thousands, even hundreds of thousands, of dollars, don't be too impressed. The players are actually betting **tournament chips.**

In virtually all tournament action, players are scrambling for final position, not for the cash value of the chips. In other words, a player with half-a-million in chips can't dash off to the casino cage and cash 'em in. The chips are merely a means of keeping score, in a sense, to determine the place of finish. That's how tournament players win money; it all depends on where they finish (where they were in the standings when they exhausted all their chips). Some major tournaments, for instance, pay up to the top 30 places.

Incidentally, it makes a big difference if a player goes out in eighth place or second place, for example. The tournament cash prizes are almost always weighted heavily toward the top three finishers. Obviously, the winner—with all the chips—wins the announced tournament prize.

• Bluffing is probably the most misunderstood element of good poker play. There are at least three different types of bluffing: A **value bluff** suggests that you have at least a modest chance of making something worthwhile out of your hand. Accordingly, this type of bluff is usually made early with more cards left to be played.

A **gut bluff** is usually a late bluff, and, as you might have already gathered, is backed up with a virtually worthless hand. You'll only win the hand if other players back down from your "make big" threat. Ideally, a gut bluff is played out against one remaining player.

And then there's the **bluff-a-bluff,** as I like to call it. Again, this one is usually made late in the betting rounds and involves two players, each trying to get the other player to fold up the tent. But what's interesting about this one is that both hands are highly vulnerable.

Incidentally, if you're ever caught in a bluff, my advice is to nod a smile and get out of the game. The advice reminds me of some old stocks I used to own.

The worst thing to do when your pants are down is to keep chuggin'. Bow out gracefully and do nothing else that would make the incident stick in a player's mind.

• **Tells** are actions, especially subtle movements, made by players that can indicate the strength, or weakness, of their hands. Most rookie players exhibit tells in the act of bluffing, which is why few can successfully pull it off. But tells can be read at any time. Do your eyes light up when you see the card you need? Or does your chin drop when you *don't* get the right card?

Many of the pros learned about their own tells by having other pros watch them. It's hard for most players to detect their own tells. Some will even go to the extreme of video taping a session. The pros who play on television always tape the programs to not only look for other players' tells, but for their own, too.

• Poker has its own language. A **boat,** a shortened version of "full boat," is slang for a full house. **Trips** is short for triplets, or three-of-a-kind. **Cowboys** are kings, **ladies** are queens, and **paint** refers to any of the face cards. The **nuts** is a hand that no one can beat. But if you're **drawing dead,** there is no way you can win regardless of the card you draw. If you **draw out,** you made a winning hand out of a modest hand. If you lost a great hand to an even greater hand, you were the victim of a **bad beat.** (These terms, and more, can be found in the glossary that ends this chapter.)

• There are many different terms for folding: You can **dump** your hand, **muck** your hand, or lay down your hand, although the latter term is mostly used as a noun: **laydown.** If someone said you made a good laydown, it means that folding was the superior move.

And there's nothing wrong with simply saying "I'm out." The problem is that most rookie players don't say it often enough. They think they're in the game to fight. They'll learn quickly. Poker isn't a boxing match; it's a game of strategy *and* common sense.

Smart Advice

Poker room managers know the games inside and out. Their wisdom in understanding the right moves at the Hold 'em tables and their willingness to help new players are highlighted in the following tips from many of the top poker room managers across the country. Heed their advice.

New players don't protect their hands. They either forget to, or they don't know how. Put your hand on the table directly in front of you and protect it with a chip marker (one of your chips) placed on top of your cards. **Otherwise, if another player throws his cards away and they land on your cards, you have a dead hand.**

Vito, poker room supervisor,
Ameristar Casino, Kansas City, MO.

Betting out of turn is a problem I see. By jumping ahead, a player could force someone to fold. And some players do it on purpose to intimidate a player to drop out of the game. Something else beginners should know: **A card dropped on the floor is dead.** Drop 'em both, you lose 'em both. Technically, you're not out of the game, you can still play the flop, but why?

> Ray, pit manager,
> Bally's, Atlantic City, NJ.

If a player needs to leave the table to eat, we give up to 30 minutes. But for any other reason our rules are a little different: If the button goes around the table three times, we page. If the player doesn't answer, the seat is given up. **When a player takes a break, the player's chips must stay on the table. If the chips are picked up, the player has lost his seat.** We're "table stakes" here. So taking stakes off the table ends the play. We're also very personalized with players, having only five tables. I always suggest that beginners find a smaller room like ours where they can be helped their first time out.

> Dick, poker room supervisor,
> Atlantis Casino, Reno, NV.

Poker is like an investment. Always protect your investment—your cards *and* your money—by managing it wisely. Only play the best value hands, either in live games (limit hold 'em) or even no-limit, where the blinds can sometimes force you to play weaker hands. But, depending on how much you have in front of you in a no-limit game, you can still bet value hands much of the time. And **know the players you're going up against,** especially if your "best value hand" is weaker than you would like.

> Eric, poker room manager,
> Arizona Charlies, Las Vegas, NV.

I see it all the time: Beginners, even veterans, complain that they're running bad, and they blame it on bad luck. So I pose this question to them: Are you sure you're good enough? Maybe you need to improve your game... statistics, emotions, the psychological part of the game. **If you continually lose, don't try to convince yourself you're just unlucky.** That's a dangerous cop-out. You're kidding yourself. You need a certain temperament, a certain discipline for gambling. And you need patience. Do you have these qualities?

Kamell, poker room shift manager,
Bellagio, Las Vegas, NV

Most beginners show a tendency to want to play too many hands. My advice: Be conservative. At a low-limit game, good starting hands are paramount because it's hard to bluff. In the long run, better players win because they play better starting hands. Incidentally, **the worst hand is 2-7 off-suit, the lowest hand (without an ace) with no straight possibilities.** The worst starting hand is hard to say... depends on the game, who's in the game, whether you're winning or losing, that sort of thing. Tell your readers to keep records of results of play of certain hands, and win/loss records, too. You can really learn from your notes.

Jack, poker lead floor,
Bicycle Casino, Bell Garden, CA.

Patience is most important. **New players think two bucks isn't much; next thing you know, you're "two-bucked" to death.** It's frustrating in low-limit games that everyone plays out their cards, so you better wait for a good hand. We get better players at 4-8, but you know what? You still need good hands. I tell beginners that just because you have two suited cards, two hearts for example, it doesn't necessarily mean it's a good hand. It's interesting to note, too, that we have six tables going, and they're all Texas Hold 'em. A couple of stud games might go, but everyone wants to play Hold 'em!

Deanna, poker room manager,
Cactus Pete's, Jackpot, NV

To play in a small tournament is better than a limit game for beginners because you get to start with more chips. For a $35-buy-in, players get $1,500 in chips and valuable experience that could last for several sessions. Playing with your own money at a limit game could end up costing a player many times that amount. Our $35-buy-in tournaments have five tables, that's 55 players (11 players at a table), and we pay the top four places. Bigger tournaments, like our $100-buy-in, pays 15 places.

Brenda, pit manager,
Chinook Winds Casino, Lincoln City, OR

There's nothing more fun than pushing out all of your chips and doubling up in a tournament game. We do a lot of $25-buy-in, no-limit tournaments which get you a thousand in chips. A ten-dollar "re-buy" gets you another thousand. Tournaments last about five hours and are much different from a "structured" limit game.

My advice: **During the first three or four rounds, hang low... tournaments are a process of elimination, so let the field bust each other out.** Then the cream comes to the top and you have to start playing some good poker. Don't get caught up in burning off your chips early.

James, poker room manager,
Colorado Belle Casino, Laughlin, NV

First, get a Texas Hold 'em computer game; play on that for a while because it's the easiest way to learn without losing money. Then, once you feel comfortable with the game, go to a casino and play in a live game, a low-limit game like 2-4. Or, try a 1-2 blind, no-limit hold 'em game because that's what everyone's looking for. There are no betting limits, but you only have to start with a $2 call of the big blind. It's the same action of a big tournament, but no big risk. It's table stakes, minimum buy-in is $50, most players go in for $100 to $200. Low-limit tournaments, no-limit action, are good for beginners, too. Internet gambling is OK, but get experience first on the computer game.

Brad, acting day-shift supervisor,
Gold Strike Casino, Tunica, MS

Players come in expecting a no-limit game, that's all they see on TV, but we have a lot of structured limit games too, occasionally a no-limit game, or a pot-limit game (where you can bet up to what's in the pot). We get some players who try 7-card stud games, but mostly the beginners want Texas Hold 'em because it's faster, a lot of action, and it's what they see on TV. Some beginners, though, who sit down at a stud game, like it. They have to play their own hand, and they like that. My advice, though, is to play what you're looking for; **don't try a different game you might not know just because a seat's open.**

Alberto, Poker room supervisor,
Harrah's East Chicago Casino, East Chicago, IN.

Believe it or not, we see players come in who don't even know the ranking of the hands. They don't know what hands to play or fold. They're coming here prematurely; every day we have to help teach these beginners how to play, and we don't mind doing that at all. TV tournaments sometimes give new players the wrong impression… the misbehavior of some pros, for example, is the worst thing. **Players need to know game etiquette.** They can't run around the tables and act like kids. They want to be like the pros, but sometimes we have to calm them down.

Doc, Poker room supervisor,
The Nugget, Sparks, NV

Incidentally, many of the poker room managers I talked to couldn't believe the number of new players who walk in with a completely distorted view of the rules of the game. They've been playing in private games with their friends, making up a lot of their own rules, and then they step into a structured casino game and feel totally lost.

Speaking for many of the poker experts, the advice is clear: Learn the game from the outset the *right* way. And even though all the managers I spoke with indicated that they are more than happy to help out beginners, it's clearly incumbent on all new players to learn the game first, maybe practicing on a computer game as one manager mentioned, and, perhaps most important, forging an intimate relationship with a good poker book.

Experience in a live game is an absolute must. But first, get the knowledge you need to make the most of that experience.

The Language Of Poker

If you're going to play Hold 'em, you should learn the terms that are commonly used. Poker has its own language. If you use the wrong terms, or ask what a particular term means, you're giving yourself away as a rookie.

Accordingly, I've done more in this chapter than just define the terms. I've elaborated on many of them so that you fully understand not only what they mean, but how to use them.

Ace kicker: A hand that includes an ace and a pair.

Ace-high: (1) A hand that includes an ace, but no pair or better. (2) A straight, flush, or straight flush with an ace serving as the highest card in the hand.

Aces up: A hand that includes two pairs, one of which is two aces.

Action: (1) A term used in all gambling endeavors to mean simply "in the game," (in action). (2) The term can also mean the amount or degree of betting ("The action was furious!")

Advertise: (1) A deceptive practice of bluffing with the intention of showing your weak hand. (2) Any intentional action on the part of a good player to suggest inexperience.

All the way: In a table-stakes game, a dealer will announce "all the way" when all players are all-in and all betting rounds have not been completed. The remaining rounds will be dealt "all the way" through since no betting is possible.

All-in: A situation where all of a player's money is in the pot.

Ante: A bet made by all players before the cards are dealt to ensure action. (2) The term can also refer to the number of chips or amount of money to make up the ante. (3) The term can also refer to the procedural aspect of making this bet.

Back in: Similar to a check-and-raise, a player "comes back into the betting" after first checking. Usually, the player simply calls a bet or raises. If the player raises, the action is a "check and raise." Both motives are somewhat deceptive because the player is assumed to be holding a decent hand. But it could be a ruse.

Backdoor: In general, a backdoor refers to a hand that a player was not trying to make. Usually, the backdoor hand is a flush or straight when the player, at the outset, appeared destined for a high pair, maybe two pair, at best. Most often, the better hand is made on the last two deals.

Bad beat: The act of getting beat with a strong hand… by a stronger hand. Not a fun thing. The only consolation is a chance to win a bad-beat jackpot that many casinos offer. And I'm not talking boobie prizes. Some casinos offer seats in big tournaments in lieu of cash prices.

Bankroll: The money that poker players carry for the purpose of buying into games. Seasoned players think of each buy-in as a "session," which may end early or late, depending on the player's fortunes. To protect a bankroll, smart gamblers set a loss limit for each session. It's not wise, however, to set limits on your winnings, being careful not to play your winnings into losses.

Belly buster: Sometimes called a "gutshot," these terms refer to a player's hope of filling an inside straight. For example, if a player's pocket cards are 10-J, and the 7 and 8 are "on the board," only a 9 will "fill" the straight.

Big blind: (1) A forced bet (to ensure action) made by the player who is two positions left of the dealer button. The big blind is posted (made) before any cards are dealt. In limit games, the amount of this bet is usually the lower of the two betting limits. In a $4-$8 game, the big blind is $4. (2) The term may also refer to the player who is in that position.

Blank: A card of no value to a player.

Blinds: See "big blind" or "small blind."

Bluff: A deceptive maneuver whereby a player bets on a weak hand as if the hand is strong. Bluffs are rarely used in low-limit games because the stakes are not high enough to make other players ponder the risk of staying in the game.

Board: (1) Another term for the "community cards" placed face up in the middle of the table for all players to use. (2) The center area of the table where the community cards are placed.

Boat: A shortened version of "full boat," a slang term for "full house" such as three 9s and two kings.

Bring it in: To start the betting. In the first betting round, the third player to the left of the dealer button is the first to have the option of betting.

Burn: To remove a card or cards from the top of the deck by a dealer before any cards are dealt to the players or to the board.

Button: A small plastic disk usually with the word *Dealer* printed across, used in games where a casino dealer is employed, and player position relative to the dealer is significant. The button rotates clockwise around the table after each hand so that all players can "act" as the dealer, thus allowing all players to experience all betting positions.

Buy the card: To call a bet simply because you want to see the next card.

Buy-in: (1) The establishment of a stake, almost always in chips, at the beginning of, and specifically for, a particular game. The term is easily confused with "bankroll." A buy-in is generally much less than a player's total bankroll for the session. (2) Casinos also use the term *buy-in* to mean the cost for entering a tournament.

Call: Making a bet equal to a previous player's bet. If a player elects not to call, or raise, the only other option is to fold the hand.

Cards speak: A rule typical of all card rooms to protect players from announcing their hands incorrectly. Dealers are always on the alert to make sure a hand is what the player says it is. Most often, a player who makes an incorrect announcement has overlooked a higher hand. The highest hand is played, regardless of how a player announced it.

Cash out: To quit a game and then cash in your chips. Of all the disciplines to follow, cashing out at the right time should be high on your list; but it's low on the list of reckless players.

Chase: Players are "chasing the cards" when they suspect that another player(s) has a better hand but they continue in the game in the hope of drawing the right cards against steep odds.

Check-raise: To check and later raise within the same betting round. Of course, in order to raise, another player must bet after you've checked. A player who plans to check and raise, usually with a strong hand, is "milking" other players into the pot and then bumping them up more. It's a sly tactic that is not allowed in some games.

Check: (1) To check is not to bet. Beginning with the second betting round, a player can check when first to act or if previous players have checked. (2) A "check" is casino parlance for "chip."

Close to the chest: (1) Timid, conservative betting. (2) A fear among many players that other players might have seen their cards. Thus, such players would hold their cards "close to the chest." Now a cliche.

Community cards: The five cards dealt face up to the middle of the table that may be used by all players in making their best hands.

Chip: A 1–5/8" round plastic disk that serves as cash at the tables. They come in various color-coded denominations. Chips are used because they are easier to work with than cash. The problem, however, is that chips tend to distort values, looking more like play-money than *real* money.

Consolidation of tables: In most tournaments, when the number of remaining players dwindles, the tables are "consolidated" in order to expedite the run to the final table. This saves dealer expenses and helps to confine the action to fewer tables as the tournament progresses.

Cowboys: A slang term for kings.

Deuce: A slang term for a 2, also known as "2-spot."

Draw out: Making a winning hand out of a so-so hand, usually with the last card.

Drawing dead: A predicament whereby a player can't possibly win the hand, regardless of the draw.

Ducks: Casino jargon for a pair of 2s in the pocket. (Not to mention a pair of 2s at the dice table— a hard 4.)

Dump: To fold a hand.

Early position: Usually one of the first three betting positions (after the blinds in the first betting round).

Fifth Street: The last community card; also known as "the river."

Flop: The first three community cards, dealt all at once in the second betting round. Also used as a verb: "The dealer flopped a queen-ace-6."

Flush: Any five cards of the same suit.

Fold: To drop out of a hand by surrendering your cards. If you do not call or raise a bet, you must fold your hand.

Four-flush: Any four cards to a flush. If you have two hearts in the pocket and see two more hearts on the flop, you have a four-flush.

Four-of-a-kind: Four cards of the same value, such as four aces.

Fourth Street: The second to last of the five community cards; the first card to hit the board after the flop; also known as "the turn."

Free card: Usually associated with the last two betting rounds—if all players check, the dealer turns over a "free" card. There were no bets to call, so the card did not "cost" the players.

Full house: Three-of-a-kind and a pair.

Garbage: A hand with no pair or better. Most often, such a hand is void of any high card. If you haven't seen garbage before, this is what it looks like: 3-5-9-2-7 (off-suit, of course).

Gimmick: You don't hear the term very much anymore, but if you do, look out! It means that a player is using a cheating method to win. A common term for a player using a gimmick is *mechanic*. Yes, it still happens, even in the better poker rooms. Incidentally, a mechanic could also be a dealer, but that's so unlikely in today's highly regulated casinos, particularly the major resort casinos and poker clubs. The theory, however, is that a dealer could be working in collusion with a player to help ensure a big win, and then later sharing in the profits.

Giving your hand away: A more common way to say it is "tipping your hand," but it doesn't necessarily mean literally showing another player your cards; the term refers to some careless action, or words spoken, on the part of a player that "gives your hand away." A good rule to follow is to use an economy of words at the poker tables.

Grifter: (1) A cheat. (2) A person without formal education (exhibiting low intellect), yet successful in spite of these shortcomings.

Hand: This simple word has multiple meanings. (1) Your held cards. (2) The best five-card ranking you can make from your pocket cards and community cards. (3) From start to completion of all the betting rounds. "I'm going to stay in for one more hand."

(4) Synonymous with "game." (Casino personnel use the term *game* to mean one betting event.)

Heads up: (1) A game with only two players. (2) A hand that is down to two players. Another term for "heads up" is "one-on-one."

Hole cards: In Hold 'em, the hole cards are the two pocket cards dealt face down to each player. In any poker game, a hole card is a card unseen by other players. Similar term are *down* and *under.* "He had aces in the hole." "He had aces under." "He had aces down."

In the money: A player in a tournament is said to be "in the money" when he or she makes it to the final table, where all nine positions win a portion of the "purse." In some cases, a "money position" can occur before the final table; in other cases, not all players at the final table win a share of the prize money.

Inside straight: A hand with four cards to a straight, usually needing an "interior" card to fill, such as 3-4-5-7. The interior card needed to make the straight is a 6. Since an inside straight suggests that only one card is needed to fill, that needed card could also be on the end of only two possible 4-to-a-straight hands: J-Q-K-A and A-2-3-4. The term *inside straight* is often used with the verb *draw:* "He's drawing to an "inside straight."

Jackpot: A casino promotion offering prize money for selected high hands or other rare occurrences. As an example, a particular "bad beat" (losing a high hand to an even higher hand) could be a prize winner. Some jackpots are "progressive," meaning that the amount to win is continually increasing until a winner is declared.

Kicker: In Hold 'em, a high card in your hand that may be needed to back up a pair. "They both had a pair of 10s, but Jim's ace kicker won the pot."

Ladies: Poker jargon for "queens." Generally, the term is reserved for a pair.

Late position: One of the last three betting positions (the player on the button, and the two players to the right of the button). In late position, a player has a distinct advantage because other players have already acted on their hands.

Laydown: Another term for "fold," although "laydown" is generally used in later betting rounds when a player folds a decent hand in fear of another player's developing hand that could be stronger.

Limit: In a limit game, bets and raises are restricted to specific amounts. For example, in a $2-$4 game, all bets and raises during the first two rounds must be $2. All bets and raises during the final two rounds must be $4.

Limp in: A term only occasionally heard to mean simply calling the "big blind." If no other players called, the big blind wins the small blind. "He limped in to see the flop."

Live hand: A player has a live hand until folded or lost. Occasionally, players need to be reminded that it's their turn, forgetting they had a live hand.

Lock: Holding the best possible hand; synonymous with the term *nuts*.

Low stakes: A term that means different limits to different players. Clearly, a $2-$4 game is low stakes. But is a $10-$20 game low stakes, too? For some; not for others.

Muck: Another term for "fold," and for the discard pile.

No limit: A Hold 'em game with no prearranged betting structure. In No-Limit Hold 'em, a player can wager up to the full amount they have in front of them.

Nuts: You have "the nuts" if you have a hand that no one can beat. Same as "lock." Say the board shows A-9-8-K-5. If you hold a 6-7, you've made your straight and nobody can beat you since no higher straight is possible and the next highest hand is 4-of-a-kind. Without a pair on the board, there is no chance of 4-of-a-kind.

Off-suit: Cards of different suits, such as jack of clubs and king of diamonds.

On the end: The river card; the last card dealt to the board.

Open-ended straight: A hand of 4-to-a-straight, whereby one of two cards can make the straight. In the more typical case, the four cards held are consecutive and do not include an ace. With a hand of 5-6-7-8, either a 4 or a 9 will make the straight. Many players overlook such a hand as 4-6-7-8-10. It is also an open-ended straight, in the sense that one of two cards can make the straight, even though both cards are "interior cards," not "end" cards. The straight can be made 4-5-6-7-8, or 6-7-8-9-10.

Outs: The number of cards yet to be seen that can improve your hand. If you are holding an open-ended straight, and none of the cards on the board can fill it for you, you have eight outs, assuming there's at least one inning, uh, betting round to go.

Overcard: A card on the board that is higher than either of your pocket cards, suggesting that another player could have at least a pair that could beat you, even if you pair up one of your pocket cards in a later draw.

Paint: The face cards: jack, queen, and king.

Pocket cards: The two cards dealt (face down) to a player; also known as "hole" cards.

Pocket pair: If both "pocket" cards are of the same value, such as two jacks, you have a "pocket pair."

Post: To put in the ante or blinds prior to the deal of the cards.

Pot limit: A limit set on any bet or raise based on the amount of money in the pot at that time. Pot limit is the least common among the three accepted forms of betting structure. The other two are simply "limit," and "no limit."

Rack: A plastic tray used to carry your chips from the cashier to the table. A rack holds five stacks of 20 chips. Incidentally, never play "out of the rack." When you get to the table, remove the chips and stack them in front of you.

Rake: The amount of money drawn from each pot by the casino dealer, either a fixed amount or a percentage, that serves as the casino's profit for running the game.

Rebuy: A player's option during a tournament to buy more chips. Usually one rebuy is allowed within a certain time frame. Many tournaments do not offer rebuys.

River: The last community card dealt. Also known as fifth street.

Rock: A player who only stays in with strong pocket cards and, even then, exhibits overly conservative play. "Rocks" do not particularly like tournaments where the blinds are continually raised, because if you don't bet very often, the blinds will eat up your chips.

Roll: (1) To turn a card or cards face up. An old term, but still in use today. (2) A shortened form of the word *bankroll*.

Royal flush: The highest poker hand in Hold 'em. A-K-Q-J-10 of the same suit. Also known as an ace-high straight flush. Since there are only five community cards and only two pocket cards, it's impossible that two players could hold a royal flush at the same time.

Satellite: A Hold 'em tournament designed primarily as a means of entry to a larger tournament. The cost of entry is minimal compared to the major tournament you would like to enter.

Set: A poker hand of three-of-a-kind in which two of the three cards are pocket cards (hole cards) and the other card of the set is a community card (on the board). It is incorrect to refer to any three-of-a-kind as a "set." Since two of the three cards are hidden, a "set" is usually a strong, deceptive hand.

Shootout: A tournament where there is no consolidation of tables, and a winner is decided from each table. These winners proceed to another table (or tables) until only one winner remains at a final table holding all the marbles. Shootouts give a player the opportunity to play against a full table, then progressively fewer players, down to a one-on-one confrontation. Since poker strategy changes as the number of players change, a shootout is a truer test of the players' abilities by forcing them to continually alter their strategies.

Short-handed: A Hold 'em game with fewer than five players.

Showdown: A comparison of the full hands of all active players at the end of the final betting round to determine the winner of the pot.

Slow-playing: A deceptive playing strategy whereby a player has a strong hand yet plays it as if it's a weak hand by checking or just calling bets. The purpose of this strategy is to pull out bigger bets on later betting rounds. It should be noted that this tactic can often backfire. A similar term is *sandbagging*.

Slow-roller: A player who holds the winning hand, yet, through facial expressions and mannerisms, let's another player think that he or she has won the pot. Then, just as that player reaches for the chips, the slow-roller shows the winning hand, usually with a smirky smile. Few poker players have the patience for this kind of childish behavior.

Small blind: (1) A forced bet (to ensure action) made by the player who is one position left of the dealer button. The small blind is posted (made) before any cards are dealt. In limit games, the amount of this bet is usually one-half of the big blind. (2) The term may also refer to the player who is in that position.

Soft-playing: A play made for the benefit of another player or players; typically seen when close friends or relatives are playing at the same table. It's not uncommon for some players to soft-play (go easy) on players who are down on their luck. It should be noted, however, that this sometimes altruistic act is not fair to other players who are not on the receiving end of such generosity. A commonly heard excuse is that a soft play was unintentional. Still, many poker players will bow out of a table if they find out or suspect that two or more players are close relatives. No one wants to play against a team.

Spot-card: Any card other than a face card or ace. Count the spots and use the old poker players' jargon: a 4-spot, a 5-spot, and so on.

Spread: To show your hand at the "showdown."

Square-up: A responsibility of dealers to ensure that each player has equal and sufficient room to play. Most Hold 'em tables will seat 10 or 11 players, but—many players will agree—only 9 players *comfortably*. If you believe that an adjacent player is moving in on your space, ask the dealer to square-up the table.

Standoff: Two identical high hands that share the pot equally.

Stealing the blinds: The act of raising on the first round of betting in the hope of making all the other players fold, and you win the blinds.

Straight: Five cards in consecutive order, not all of the same suit. If they are all suited (the same suit), the hand is called a "straight flush."

Suited: Cards of the same suit, such as jack and king of spades.

Sympathy show: At a showdown, a player with a losing hand shows it because it was a strong hand.

Table stakes: A limit set on a game whereby players can bet only what's "on the table." You can't go into your pocket for more ammo. At least that's the rule in a casino-run game. In a hotel-room game, you can probably bet your Rolex! If that's not enough, there's always that deed to the lost gold mine.

Tell: A motion, a twitch, a nervous habit—however subtle—broadcast by a player for other players to read. The idea is that tells can signal the strength, or weakness, of the subject player's hand. A tell can be as simple as a raised eyebrow, or as complicated as a series or pattern of glances.

Toke: Also called a "tip" or "gratuity," it's given to a dealer by any player, not necessarily a winner. Tips can become a significant drain on some players who simply go overboard with their gratuities. Players may unknowingly "double-tip" in cases where a percentage of the pot is automatically held out for the dealer.

There is no rule that says you must tip a dealer, but it is common courtesy to do so, especially if you're a winner and the dealer has been friendly and courteous. Just remember to tip in moderation.

Trips: Poker slang, short for "triplets." If you have "trips," you have 3-of-a-kind.

Turn: The first community card dealt after the flop. Also known as Fourth Street.

Winner Take All: A tournament concept whereby the sole winner either wins all the chips or wins the announced prize. There is no prize distribution for second-place, third-place and so-on finishes. This form of tournament is disliked by a multitude of players, and, accordingly, does not usually draw well. Early World Series Of Poker tournaments were winner-take-all.

Woolworth: Of all the old poker jargon, little of which is used today, this one is still a popular favorite. If you have a "Woolworth," you've got a pair of 5s and a pair of 10s. That's right; five and dime.

World Series Of Poker: The mother lode of all poker tournaments, held each spring at Binion's Horseshoe in downtown Las Vegas, but being challenged today by several major resort-casinos. Binion's, incidentally, is now owned by Harrah's.

Chapter 4

Horse Racing

The horse-racing industry has perked up somewhat over recent years, especially at major tracks.

It was not that long ago that many of the minor tracks around the country had closed up, sold to developers who saw more value in the land than in the track itself. And for those tracks that stayed open, bettors complained about small fields of horses. Some races would go off with only five or six horses running, but they did go off. That beat betting on bulldozers clearing the way for a housing development.

Bettors don't like small fields of horses because that usually means small prices. It was a hand-me-down problem; there were fewer horses in the races because there were fewer horses foaled. Breeders had seen the signs and simply were not producing as they used to.

It all boiled down to attendance, which dwindled through much of the '90s. Sadly, there was a one-word answer as to why: Attrition. You would see fewer young couples at the tracks back then. Most of the patrons were senior citizens, brought up on horse racing during its glory years of the '50s and '60s. It remains tough today to attract the young players who want more excitement for their gambling dollars, but it's happening, albeit a slow process of recovery.

Actually, there are several marketing moves underway to further attract new players, but one in particular doesn't really bode well for the sport. The racing industry, in its divine wisdom, has come up with a one-word solution: Slot machines! OK, two words. Sure, slots will bring in tons of players! Tons of *slot* players! Slot players who couldn't care less about who's racing in the eighth. For those tracks that have already tried this weird cross-marketing of two competitive "sports," the results are in:

Says a slot player: "I like the slots, but I don't like it when the races go off. It bothers my concentration." Says a track owner: "I don't want a racetrack with slot machines. I want slot machines with a racetrack."

It's a commentary I would prefer to spare you, but if I'm going to talk to you about betting horses, you need to know what's going on. Now you've got the picture.

The Two "Pluses"
Of Horse Racing

Compared to the casino scene, horse racing is a slow game: two minutes of exciting racing followed—and preceded by—30 minutes of waiting. A period when the old-timers are studying the next race. But younger players, for the most part, balk at the notion of studying a racing form.

Can you imagine going to the casino to play blackjack, burying your head in a blackjack book for half an hour before you plunk down each bet?

Well, horse racing is obviously different from blackjack, and this "negative" really isn't one at all. A track-junky I know calls it "stake preservation." And he's right. You can have an exciting afternoon of thoroughbred racing (or a fun night at the harness track) and make maybe a dozen bets at the most.

Which leads us to the other "plus" of horse racing: low risk, high rewards. With only a few dollars at risk, you can take your best shots with the potential for huge payoffs! As you'll soon learn, there are short-odds and long-odds bets that you can make, and we're going to concentrate on the relatively longer odds of what the track calls "exotic" wagering. But there's nothing exotic about it at all. In fact, these popular bets you are about to learn are the real lure of the track. It's just that we're going to make these bets a bit differently than most handicappers do, in the hope of beating the odds and walking away with fistfuls of money!

Study Hall

What's fun for some is not fun for others. Poring over racing statistics for 20 minutes out of every half-hour is a negative in the minds of many of the few beginners who come along... and it's a negative that I want to try to eliminate for you. But it's a biggie; it's the "studying" part of the game. You can't just pick horses on a whim; you're supposed to study what is called a "racing form" (or a "program" at the harness tracks), which contains the "past performances" of the horses.*

I'm not a proponent of spending untold hours behind a pair of reading glasses with a racing form clutched tightly in one's grip. It works for some, but it doesn't seem to work for the new players. Not many of them, anyhow.

Over 500 horse-racing books have been published over the years, but few of them are actually about horse racing. The purpose of these books is to show you—in 384 pages—how to read a racing form. That's right. Inside these books are all the tips you need to find something in "the form" that has—incredibly—escaped all the other handicappers.

For each day of racing at every thoroughbred track around the country, the racing form provides a record of each horse's recent races. An information sheet, if you will, of detail after detail, so you can produce a "system" for picking winners.

Let's see, bet the horse that's still a maiden (hasn't won its first race), that's not a shipper (shipped in from a different track), that races well on grass (horses race on both turf and dirt), that gained in the last quarter (didn't quit in the stretch), that has dropped in class (racing for a smaller purse), that drew an inside post (close to the rail), that finished in-the-money in its last outing (2nd or 3rd, in this case), not coming off a turn-out (has recently raced), that is racing a longer distance (a route vs. a sprint), that carries the same jockey (the short guy in the clown-suit with the whip).

If you're like me, and not that interested in putting this much effort into handicapping, but you still think you would like to go to the races, you're in luck. **I'm going to show you a way to bet horses *without* studying! Without even *buying* a racing form. You won't *need* a racing form!** The other handicappers will make your decisions for you. But not just the regulars. You'll learn how to detect what the *smart* handicappers are doing. Then *you* can do it, too! There's nothing like having someone else do your homework for you!

The Basics

I'm going to assume that you know little, if anything, about the mechanics of horse racing, so the next several pages will be devoted to the basics of wagering. It's not complicated; I'm going to give you a crash course. This will be like cramming for an exam. A lot of information in a few paragraphs.

Pencils ready. Here goes:

There are usually nine or ten races on the program at a thoroughbred track. Harness tracks might have as many as 13 races.

Most thoroughbred races are scheduled every 30 minutes. Harness races rarely have more than 20 minutes between them.

Thoroughbred races are different lengths, from a mile and three-eighths to six furlongs. A **furlong** is one-eighth of a mile, so a six-furlong race is three-quarters of a mile. The longer races are called **routes**. Shorter races are called **sprints**. Virtually all harness races today are one mile in length.

Harness-racing horses are called "standardbreds," and are either **pacers** or **trotters**. The difference is in the gait: A pacer "paces" by moving both the front and rear leg of one side simultaneously. A trotter "trots" by moving a front leg and opposite rear leg simultaneously. If a standardbred **breaks** into a gallop, the horse must be "pulled up" and placed by the driver at the end of the field.

Most races are either an **allowance race** or a **claiming race.** An allowance race (called a "conditioned race" at the harness tracks) states certain conditions for which a horse can be eligible, such as purse money earned, number of races won, and age or sex of the horse. For example, a race might be conditioned as, "Fillies and mares, non-winners of 4 races lifetime." In the case of thoroughbreds, an allowance race may also include additional weights to carry relative to purse earnings. A claiming race is for horses that may be bought (claimed) by any licensed racehorse owner for a specific claiming price. There are also **stakes** races in which the owners of the horses pay a fee to be entered.

You can bet a horse to **win** (finish first), **place** (finish first or second), or **show** (finish first, second, or third). You can also bet an **exacta** by picking the two horses that will finish first and second, in order. Some harness tracks use the term **perfecta** instead of exacta. A **quinella** is just like an exacta except the horses do not have to finish in exact order. A **trifecta** is just like the exacta except you must pick the *three* horses that will finish first, second, and third, in order. To win the **daily double,** you must pick the winners of the first and second race. Some tracks now offer a second daily double later in the program.

The minimum bet you can make is two dollars. There is no maximum limit because all bets are **parimutuel,** meaning that the winning bets are all paid from the total of all bets made for that race, called a **pool**. The track does not bank the bets as a casino does; instead, it takes a certain percentage of money from each pool, called a **takeout,** to pay purses and overhead and make a profit.

The more money that is bet on a particular horse, the lower the **odds** (the payoff expressed as odds to one, such as 3 to 1. The odds continually change as bets are made, and are displayed on a **Totalizator,** a large, lighted, scoreboard-like panel usually installed in front of the grandstand. TV monitors installed throughout the grandstand and clubhouse also display the odds.

The amount of money you win, therefore, depends on how many other players also won. If you were among many winners because the **favorite** (the horse with the lowest odds) won, you will win only a token amount. If, however, you picked a winning **long-shot,** a horse with higher odds because few other players made bets on this same horse, your winning ticket will be worth much more.

After each race, the Totalizator will display the **prices,** the values of winning tickets. The prices are all based on a two-dollar wager and include the return of this theoretical two-dollar bet. So, to convert the prices to odds, simply subtract two and divide by two.

Totalizator displays these prices:

	WIN	PLACE	SHOW
1ST	8.00	4.20	2.80
2ND		3.00	2.40
3RD			2.20

$8.00 TO WIN converted to odds to 1:
Simply subtract $2 and divide by 2:

Win $8
       −2
       6   Divided by 2 equals 3 (3 to 1 odds)

You will win three times the amount of your wager, and your wager will be returned to you. If you wagered $5, you will win $15 and collect $20.
If you simply add one to the odds—in this case, 4—that number will tell you how much you will collect (4 times your wager).

This simple formula saves a lot of grief trying to determine exactly how much you won with, say, a $15 ticket (3 x $15 = $45 *in winnings*).

Many handicappers do it the "old-fashioned" way and divide the amount of the ticket by $2 and then multiply by the price, $8 in our example ($7.50 x 8 = $60 *to collect*).

But my easier way has another advantage of showing you exactly what the odds were at the **post** (at the time the race went off). And it follows the casino standard of quoting payoffs in "odds to one."

All tracks provide at least a basic program that gives you information about each race that day, including a rundown of the horses entered, their **post position** (the gate from which the horse leaves—the 1st post, also called the 1-hole, is closest to the rail), the name of the jockey, and, of key importance, the **morning line.** A track handicapper assigns odds to the field of horses in each race, which becomes the morning line, also known as the "opening line," or "program odds." Based on these early odds, the track handicapper will also list the horses he or she believes will finish 1st, 2nd, and 3rd. These horses are referred to as the **program picks,** and usually carry considerable influence among bettors.

The horses' post-position number is clearly displayed on the **saddle cloth** of the horse so that you can identify a particular horse during the race. A standardbred, however, also uses a **head number** because sometimes the harness equipment obscures the number on the "saddle" cloth.

Another important distinction between thorough-breds and standardbreds is the way the race goes off. Thoroughbreds leave from a portable **starting gate** that is fixed in a particular location on the track depending on the length of the race. The race begins when the doors to the gates all open in a quick, simul-taneous action. But at the harness track, the starting gate is not stationary; it's attached to a car equipped to hold this different kind of gate that resembles a trackwide fence. The car moves slowly at first, build-ing up speed, while the horses gradually move up to the gate. When it is determined that all the horses are "up and on the gate," the gate opens from a center hinge and swings away from the horses. The race begins as the car speeds away.

It's interesting to note that one of the track **stewards,** an official of the racing commissioner's office of that state, not an employee of the track, is seated in the car and makes the decision when to start the race. The steward continues to monitor the race from his position in the car. Most races today utilize three stewards who are responsible for the fairness of the race and for determining the official outcome. They also cite infractions by fining or suspending trainers, jockeys, and drivers, and, in some cases, by **setting down** a horse, which means moving a horse down in the official order of finish. Sometimes, a horse may be disqualified.

When you see the term **official** appear on the Totalizator, you know that the stewards have reviewed the race, concluded it was fair, and assigned the order of finish. Until the official sign is lit, the race is unofficial, even if a listing of finish appears on the board. *Always hold on to your tickets until the official sign is lit.*

When you go to a track, you will find it's a little different from going to a casino. For one, the track will charge you for parking. General parking is cheap but usually is a cab ride from the track. Preferred parking, which is closer, is expensive. Next, you'll have to buy the program, which is not cheap, either. And, if you want a racing form, that's a few more bucks, too. If you want to sit in the **grandstand,** it's open seating, but get there early for a good spot. If you would prefer a nicer surrounding, try the **clubhouse,** but you'll pay extra for this, too. How do I compare the grandstand to the clubhouse? You'll eat hot dogs in the grandstand; dine on filet mignon at your white-linen table in the clubhouse.

The procedure for actually making your bets is no big deal. But there's a perk to betting in the clubhouse, as you might expect. There are more ticket windows so you should not have to stand in long lines. Since making late bets is a crucial aspect of the way we're going to bet horses, you'll see that a clubhouse table is probably well worth the extra investment. Scribble on your program exactly what you want to bet and take the program with you to the window. Have your money ready.

There is a correct procedure for telling the ticket writer what you want. If you follow it, the whole thing will go smoother and faster. First, tell the writer the amount you want to bet, then the kind of bet, followed by the horse number. For example, if you like the 3-horse to win and you want to bet five bucks, say: **"Five dollars to win on the 3."** The writers don't want to know the name of the horse, just the number. And they push the buttons to record and print out your ticket exactly in the order I've listed. That's why it's the most efficient way to do it.

Incidentally, it's always assumed that the bet you're making is for the next race. If you're betting a later race, then begin your instruction with, "In the seventh race...."

Return to your table, take another bite of that juicy steak, sit back, and relax. Oh, and take good care of your ticket. Anyone can cash it if you lose it.

Neat Things To Know

• All horses bred for racing celebrate their birthdays on January 1st, even though most are born between April and June (some may be a month or two late of this schedule). So, for the first few months of each year, horses are a little younger than their listed age.

• Although many factors weigh in, horses generally start their racing careers as two-year-olds. It's often said that horses reach their peak performances as a three- and four-year-old.

• A horse is called a **foal** for the first three months; a **weanling** until January 1st when it becomes one year old and appropriately named a **yearling.** The foal's mother is called the **dam,** or **broodmare,** and the father is called the **sire,** or **stallion.**

• A horse is a horse, of course… unless it is a male under five years of age, in which case it is a **colt.** A **horse,** as that term is used on racing forms, refers to a male five years old or older. Any male that is "desexed," regardless of age, is called a **gelding.** A female horse under five years of age is called a **filly.** When she becomes five years old, she's a **mare.** In harness racing, the dividing line between colts and horses, and fillies and mares, is four years of age, a year less than their thoroughbred counterparts.

• One of the important measures of past-performance charts are **calls,** a listing that shows the position of a horse in a race and the lengths behind the leader at five key distances, such as 3/4 mile, 1/2 mile, 1/4 mile, and so on. The last three calls are supposed to be in the stretch run, but some charts are not specific about distance to the finish line… particularly the last 1/16 of a mile (about 100 yards). Other charts now list the last call at 1/8 of a mile. A lot can happen in that not-so-short distance; what I want to know is what happened in the last 100 yards… even 50 yards! That's why handicappers who watch race after race know more than the casual bettors. They know if a particular horse can finish because they've witnessed the "performances." A race is stretched out over the first three quarters, then the horses start to "bunch," or perhaps one or two horses come out of the pack and fight for the finish line. Remember what I'm about to tell you: The race is in that last 100 yards.

• **Horse psychologists** were the butt of jokes years ago, but not anymore. Today, their opinions at yearling sales, for example, could be worth millions! Unlike a racehorse owner or trainer, the horse psychologists (many are also vets) claim to be able to judge the most important features of a racehorse. No, not the legs or knees... not physical features... but psychological ones. They look into the heart of the racing animal to determine if it has the desire to race. Not all horses enjoy racing or even know what's going on. But there are those special horses that know what they have to do. The evidence is in the way they finish. Take it from a former racehorse owner: There are horses that tire when they've had enough, and there are other horses that run like a tailback to the end zone, expending every last ounce of energy. They know what they're supposed to do.

• If you live in the Midwest, chances are an exacta is called a **perfecta.** It's the same bet, just a different name.

• Another bet that's similar to an exacta is called a **quinella.** To win the bet, you must select the two horses that will finish 1st and 2nd, in *either* order. A $2 quinella and a $1 two-horse exacta box cost the same. But be careful... a winning quinella ticket might be worth more, or less, than half of the exacta price.

• When the track announcer says, "Hold all tickets," it usually means one of three things has happened: (1) The finish was too close to call so a **photo** needs to be developed and studied to determine the official order of finish. (2) One of the stewards in charge of the race suspects that an infraction occurred during the race so an **inquiry** is called. A review of the video tape of the race, sometimes from different camera positions, will be made. (3) One of the jockeys or drivers suspects an infraction occurred during the race so an **objection** is called, resulting in a review of the race.

• Inquiries and objections can lead to a horse being **set back** which means to be placed in a lower finish position than the unofficial finish. Depending on the severity of the infraction, a horse may also be **disqualified.**

• Once the **official** sign has been lit, or the track announcer states that the race is official, the prices that are posted on the tote board stand. Sometimes, however, subsequent action by the stewards, or the state's racing commissioner, can result in a redistribution of purse money.

• Sometimes two or more horses are coupled together as a single betting interest, called an **entry.** If the horses are owned by the same owner or trained by the same trainer, the entry is called a **mutual entry.** Horses in an entry have the same post number (such as 2 and 2A) but obviously do not leave from the same post.

• A term that seems to confuse new bettors is **mutual field.** The term simply means a grouping of horses, other than an entry, that is considered one betting interest. A mutual field is made whenever the number of horses in a race exceeds the capacity of the Totalizator. Generally, the highest number on the tote board is assigned to all the horses with that number and higher.

• There are only two exceptions to the standard rule that payment is only made to bettors for the finish of the top three horses. In one case, a **dead heat** for show (3rd) will result in four horses finishing "in the money." A dead heat means a finish for any of the top three positions resulted in a tie, because the photo was unable to discern a difference in finish. In the other case, some tracks offer a **superfecta** wager that requires you to pick the top four horses in order.

• At the harness track, there might be a **recall** just before the race has started. A recall means the race will not go and will be restarted. Some of the reasons for a recall include: a horse that will not take to the gate, a horse that interferes with another horse, a horse that falls, or a horse that displays broken equipment. If a recall is charged to a particular horse, it must not cause a second recall or it will be disqualified. A recall is never made solely because of a breaking horse.

• A ticket writer does not hand you your ticket; the machine that created the ticket hands it to you. Really. It's up to you to take it. If you don't take it, the next person in line might take it. And when you do take it, look it over immediately. If it's not written the way you want it, give it back to the ticket writer and get it exchanged. The contents of a ticket is solely your responsibility.

• The average cost today to attend a racetrack, including parking, seating, minimal food & beverage service, programs, and other forms, is nearly $20! And you still haven't made your first bet! But don't give up yet. Hopefully, the special *Smart Gambling* strategies that follow will help you recoup your costs and send you to the winner's circle!

Overview

If we were to bet horses the way most handicappers do: by studying the racing forms and programs, hanging around the track, getting to know the trainers and jockeys, etc., we would not be doing what *Smart Gambling* is all about.

Studying the forms… and I mean *really* studying… is not easy. Most newcomers would also say it is not fun. So that's not going to be a part of our strategy.

Hanging around the track… and I mean *really* hanging… is fine if you're (a) retired, (b) laid off, (c) a rich kid, or (d) a bum. But I'm assuming you're like me and actually have a job that occupies most of your time and is definitely required if you want to go out and buy groceries. So let's forget the idea of bumming around with the horses. Let's look at more sensible ways of making money at the track that better fit today's "do it now" lifestyle.

In the preceding pages, I whetted your appetite with a subtle hint as to how *Smart Gambling* would apply to horse racing. I said that we'll let other handicappers do our handicapping for us.

Incidentally, the term **handicap,** in the context of horse racing, simply means "to pick." A handicapper is someone who picks horses to win, place, show, fill up a trifecta, or whatever. If you're betting horses, you're handicapping. If you're giving out advice on which horses to bet, you're handicapping.

There are two key reasons why we can rely on someone else's picking. "Rely" might not be the best choice of words. We really can't rely on anything. Handicapping at the race track is gambling, pure and simple. Let's just say we're going to "go with the flow" of certain handicappers who are much better than we are.

The Track Handicapper: The handicapper we first want to pay attention to is called "the trackman." It may not be the politically correct term, but that's what these people have been referred to in racing programs since day one. We'll use the term **track handicapper.** It's the responsibility of the track handicapper to set a "morning line" by assigning odds to each horse in a given race. At some tracks, the morning line may be referred to as "probable odds." These odds are clearly shown on the program, representing the likelihood of a particular horse winning. As a result of the assignment of these odds, three horses are picked as the program favorites. Obviously, the program favorites are the horses with the best odds.

Most programs will identify these horses at the bottom of each racing page with the heading: Trackman's Selections. A few tracks around the country do not spell out the three top picks at all, simply leaving it up to the bettors to figure it out themselves.

I want to make sure you'll be able to accurately determine the top picks just in case the track doesn't do it for you. Odds lower than 5 to 1 can sometimes confuse inexperienced bettors. It's important that you can distinguish among the rank of odds from lowest to highest. So, here's a chart of the typical odds you'll find at the racetrack, starting with the lowest odds (best chance of winning) and reading down:

1-5	6-5	5-2
2-5	7-5	3
1-2	3-2	7-2
3-5	8-5	4
4-5	9-5	9-2
1	2	5

Odds greater than 5 to 1 are easy as pie. The odds will always be "to one," such as 6 to 1, 7 to 1, 8 to 1, and so on. As you look down your program, you'll quickly be able to tell the long-shots from the favorites, and be able to rank them as the track handicapper has done.

Of course, the program lists the horses in their order of post position, not in their order of odds. That's why you need to be able to do this simple chore.

If we're going to rely on the morning line to help us cash winning tickets, it would be nice to know exactly how accurate the line is. In other words, just exactly how good is the track handicapper?

Well, at many tracks around the country, the track handicapper is really the "secretary of racing," which means we're relying on the person whose main job is to "write" the races by listing all the conditions for eligibility. The racing secretary then puts the **race card** together. The race card is the program of races for a particular day. It might include allowance races, claiming races, or stakes races. It's up to the racing secretary to put as many horses into a race as possible, and make the card the most exciting for the bettors.

In addition, the racing secretary is also in charge of "the draw," the actual process of assigning post positions to the horses. The secretary of racing is like a "program director" of a radio station. Instead of deciding which songs will be played, he or she decides which horses will race. So, as you might imagine, this person knows the horses, the trainers, the jockeys, and the track itself about as well as anyone. A certain reliance on the track handicapper's selections just makes good sense.

Racetracks conduct ongoing reviews of the track handicapper's performance because it is important that the picks are reasonably reliable. Setting realistic odds is important to the track just as it is to the bettors in the stands.

Generally, a good track handicapper will pick the winning horse in one out of three races. With nine races on a card, the track handicapper will usually pick three winners. If the payoff for a "win" ticket would always be higher than 2 to 1, we could all quit our jobs and just hang around the racetrack. But most favorites go off at odds of 2 to 1 or less. In fact, a winning horse goes off as the "odds-on favorite" (at less than 1 to 1 odds) nearly 20 percent of the time. It's not too exciting to cash a two-dollar ticket and win a measly dollar. In fact, it's not worth the risk, either. Picking just the winning horse is not the way to make big money at the racetrack, and that's not the way we're going to do it, anyhow. But at least now you know just how good the track handicapper is. Pretty darned good.

Of course, the track handicapper doesn't just pick the winning horse. Technically, the job means picking *all* the horses, since odds must be assigned to each horse in a race. And here's where the real interesting stuff comes in. Now pay attention.

My own studies have shown that a track handicapper has an unusual tendency to select the winning horse as the 2nd- or 3rd-place pick. **In researching several of the major tracks, I've noted that the winning horse was picked 2nd or 3rd an uncanny 44 percent of the time!** Now that doesn't mean it's going to happen every time you go to the track. The track handicapper has good days and off days like everyone else. I remember one particular card at a harness track in Chicago where the winners were correctly picked in every single race! And there were twelve races that day! Now that's uncanny! But if the track handicapper can pick all the winners, he can also *miss* all the winners. And that certainly does happen.

When I first began compiling research several years ago, I studied past performances just as other handicappers at the track did, except I was looking at the track handicapper's performance while other bettors were busy studying the horses! The results of my work from that era would be seriously skewed today for several reasons.

For one, there are smaller fields of horses today, which would certainly increase the likelihood of better handicapping. But I've also found that the track handicappers of yesteryear were just plain better than those today.

Another factor that needs to be plugged in for today's track handicappers is the changing field of horses. The game of racing has become more transient today. Jockeys move around more from track to track, as do trainers and the horses in their barns. The old days of a "circuit" of horses, jockeys, and trainers moving from track to track as a meet closes and another one opens, is becoming passé. Clearly, there are factors that make it easier for the track handicapper today, but there are also factors that make it tougher.

Much of my research for this chapter has been "filtered" to reflect today's entire racing picture as best I can. For example, the bulk of my older information came from the days when I handicapped harness horses almost exclusively. In those races, the circuit was intact and the field of horses was usually eight or nine. Bettors could expect solid performance from the track handicapper, and they usually got it.

For this discussion, let's go with the track handicapper's capability of picking three winners out of nine races as a reasonable average to expect. Let's also assume that the track handicapper can find the winner within the 2nd or 3rd spots four races out of nine. So, out of nine races, the winner will come from the top three picks about seven races out of nine. An overall average over many years of research puts this number at 6.4 races out of nine, but let's go with 7 since races today are rarely filled as they were in the past. Remember this statistic because we are going to use it often in putting together our bets later on in this chapter.

Professional Handicappers: The other handicappers we want to pay attention to are in the grandstand or the clubhouse just as you and I, but with one big difference: They *do* study the forms, they *do* hang around the track, they *do* know as much, or more, than the track handicapper, and they wager big bucks to prove it. **Because "professionals" make such large wagers, we can usually pick them out of the crowd. How? By watching for significant changes in the odds as the wagers are recorded on the tote board.**

Another telltale sign is the timing of their wagers. These "pro" bettors—and that includes bettors who might have inside information—

almost always make their bets late. Why? Because they don't want to tip their hand. They know that many bettors are looking for these large swings in the odds as a signal as to which horse to bet. Unlike the stock market, a hot tip at the track brings *down* the price of a horse. The more people betting it, the lower the price.

Sometimes it's difficult to spot these sudden increases in wagering, especially at major tracks with literally thousands of bettors contributing to the tote board. Since the bets we're looking for are made late, these particular bets become a smaller percentage of the pool as the betting continues. The odds may not change as dramatically the later it gets because the percentage increase becomes less significant, so you will have to keep a keen eye on the late odds as they change. Generally, the tote board updates the odds about every five minutes.

Here's what we have so far: We're going to look for late money, late *big* money, as a tipoff to what the pros think. But we'll use this information judiciously, coupled with the information provided us by the track handicapper, in making our own selections.

There's a term I purposely didn't define for you in the preceding pages on the basics of horse racing, even though it certainly belongs under "basics." I didn't tell you about it then because I wanted to save it for when we talk about actually making bets. And now's a good time to highlight it. The term is **shut out.** It's what happens when you don't get to the window in time to make your bet. Ticket machines lock up at the start of a race. Obviously, a racetrack needs protection against accepting bets after a race has started. A bell rings at the ticket windows when the race goes off. If you're still standing in line when you hear the bell, you're out of luck.

It's an important fact to deal with, since the bets we're going to make will most often be made late. So learn which ticket writers are the most efficient. Learn to identify bettors who take too much time. Above all, make your bets from the clubhouse, where there's usually a higher ratio of ticket writers to bettors than in the grandstand.

Optimum Betting

Bettors who support themselves financially by handicapping horses have one goal in mind: to find the winning horse. They are not looking for an **overlay,** a racing term that means a better price than the horse's past performance would warrant.

I hear it all the time. A bettor says, "I don't like such-and-such a horse because the price isn't high enough." Even though the horse was carefully picked out to win, the bettor is going to continue looking because the odds were too low. It's what I call, "looking for a horse to beat the winner." The pros don't think this way at all. They find the winner, and then they bet the winner regardless of the price.

There's something else the pros don't do. They never bet a horse to place or show. Always to win. To win! No daily doubles, no perfectas, no trifectas. To win; that's their name of the game, and it should be ours, too, if we were to take the long and bumpy route to becoming a professional handicapper.

How often do you suppose they find the winning horse? You might be surprised to know that they cash only one or two tickets a day. But they may only bet two or three races! That's right. Most of the time, the pro handicapper is just watching. Picking up valuable information for future races. As a racing pro told me many years ago, "If I'm not absolutely convinced a horse is going to win, I pass."

The New Professional

By now it should be clear that the pro bettor at the horse track has the short stick among the three gambling endeavors featured in *Smart Gambling*. Whether the sports bettor or the poker player has the long stick is irrelevant and argumentative at this point since we're all in the horse-racing mode.

The pro racehorse handicappers need tons of patience to wait out the races where they have no action. And tons more patience to work their way through a past-performance chart, which, many pros now believe (this writer included), is sorely lacking in vital information. It just can't compare to watching a good workout, or following particular trainers and their stables of horses from race to race. It's no different from what we talked about earlier in the sports-betting chapter about following a particular conference of teams. No one can keep track of all the teams; no one can keep track of all the horses!

As we approach the strategies to help make you a winner at the track, understand that I consider these attacks to be professional also, but a different kind of "professional." They are professional strategies that lend a certain excitement to the win, which the old-line professionals rarely feel. And, more important, they are far less tedious.

Remember, one of the many benefits of my strategies is the simple fact that we will not be competing among the other pros, the "insider" pros in particular, but actually teaming up with them in a sense, as we search out their wagers. You're about to see exactly how this plan will play out and find out why it's important to play "follow the leader."

Why? Because many of these top handicappers are the owners and trainers (even the grooms and stablehands) of these very horses we will be betting. And it's a worthy merger, indeed! In some cases, the owners and trainers make more money betting races than winning races! I'll never forget what a horseman told me when I first got involved in this sport of the favorites and the favored. It was short but it was sweet: "I make my money at the window!"

Do you think he doesn't know when one of his horses is getting sick or coming off a bad training mile? Do you think he doesn't know when a particular horse is at its peak, fit and ready to race hard? What if he just changed to a different bit and knows he'll now get better performance? What if he just scoped one of his horses and found the solution to a breathing problem?

No one would want to play the stock market if only a few other players knew something that would boost or tumble a stock. That's why the SEC regulates stock trading; it keeps the game on an even keel. Of course, players in the stock market can usually pick up a piece of the insider's "edge" the next day just by keeping a close eye on the market. But it doesn't work that way at the track. You either know it when it counts, or it's worthless hindsight. The track won't take your bets on yesterday's races.

Smart Gambling Strategies

Remember, the optimum way of gambling is not the most exciting. The optimum way to bet horses, as you've just learned, is for a rare kind of individual. I doubt if it's you; it's certainly not me.

Rarely, for example, does the old-line professional have a shot at a high multiple-odds payoff. The wins are modest but sweet. After all, the winnings are used to pay the bills. That same pro handicapper I quoted earlier is deserving of another quote: "For me, the wins are not so much exciting as they are satisfying."

For us, we *want* excitement. We want to enjoy the sheer anxiety of chasing a dream ticket. And that dream ticket, more times than not, is a trifecta treat.

Trifecta Box

There's a better way to bet three horses in a trifecta. It's called a **trifecta box.** Let's say we "box" the 3-5-8 instead of just playing the straight ticket. Now, the horses can fill the top three spots in *any* order. Boxing three horses means you are really making six different bets. There are six different ways that three horses can finish. The ticket would cost you $12 (6 wagers at $2 each), but you can also make this bet for $1 per way, so the ticket will only cost you $6. If you win, you'll get half of the trifecta price.

The downside of a three-horse trifecta box is that you still have to pick the three horses that will finish in the top three spots. How much easier it would be if we could pick four horses, or even five, and box them. Well, we can do that, too, but it's gosh-awful expensive. A $1 trifecta box of five horses will set you back $60, and you'll only get half the pot! No. That's not our solution. A trifecta box is not the way we're going to make our wagers. But since it's a common wager at the track, I wanted you to know about it.

Incidentally, how would you like to make a bet that can't miss? How would you like a guaranteed lock to win the trifecta? Well, you can, by simply boxing *all* the horses in the race! Let's say there are eight horses racing. If you box all eight, the bet will cost you $336 for a $1 ticket ($672 for a $2 ticket). If the favorite wins, and there are no long-shots in the money (the top three spots), the trifecta might pay anywhere from $75 to $150 depending on how many other bettors also won the trifecta. It's even possible that the trifecta price would be a lowly $50 or so. If that were the case, you would have spent $336 for a $1 trifecta box that pays $25.

Of course, the race might have knocked out the favorites, allowing a long-shot to come in on top. Now that $336 ticket might look pretty good! I've seen trifecta prices as high as several thousand dollars. But is this the risk you want to take? No. Of course not. The trifecta box, no matter how many horses we plug in, is not the way to the roses.

The Trifecta Wheel

This bet confuses most new bettors, but it doesn't have to. The **trifecta wheel** is designed for handicappers who like to pick a certain number of horses to finish on top, a certain number to finish 2nd, and a certain number to finish 3rd. That's it. No big deal. But sometimes it's a little tough to figure out the cost of the ticket.

The trifecta wheel has a lot of advantages that we want to use. A typical trifecta wheel ticket has one horse picked to win (or it can be in either of the other two slots), and five other horses picked for the other two spots. A $1 ticket costs $20. A bit more reasonable but still too steep.

Another downside of this particular bet is that a certain horse you pick has to win. If that horse doesn't win, you lose. And the other two spots must be filled up by two of the remaining five horses. This still isn't what we want, but we're getting there.

The bet I like and use most often is called a **trifecta partial wheel.** Here's the basis for the bet:

We're going to pick four horses, total. Two of the horses can either win, place, or show. A third horse can either place or show, and a fourth horse can only show. That's it. We have four horses to work with. And, get this... our cost for a $1 ticket is only $8. Here's how it looks on paper:

WIN   1-2
PLACE   1-2-3
SHOW   1-2-3-4

To confirm that there are eight ways to win:

1	1	1	1	2	2	2	2
2	2	3	3	1	1	3	3
3	4	2	4	3	4	1	4

Here's the way you should think of this bet:
If the 4-horse is in the money, it must show.
If the 3-horse is in the money, it can't win.

So now we know the means to picking horses, and the ticket we want to write. All that's left is how to do the picking. After all, we can't always bet the 1-2-3-4, as in our example. We need different numbers to plug in!

Here's how we do it:

The Fine Art Of Picking Horses

On your program, mark the track handicapper's selections with a yellow highlighter by drawing through the horse's name. Now those three horses will be quickly discernible. Next, find all the horses with morning-line odds of 15 to 1 or higher and draw two diagonal lines through the listing from corner to corner with ink pen. The large "X" you'll create will be easily noted. These horses will have been eliminated from consideration.

Next, wait until nearly half of the betting period has elapsed. Typically, this is 20 to 30 minutes, so you'll be waiting no more than 10 minutes. At that time, write down the new odds from the tote board for all the horses in consideration. Most programs allow you room to do this directly beside the morning-line odds on the program. Note those horses (other than the yellow-lined picks) where the odds have been lowered. The best way of noting the horses with lowered odds is with a green highlighter. Draw a line with the highlighter directly above or below the horse's name. The length of the line will be determined as follows: the lower the drop in odds and the longer into the betting period, the longer the line.

As the race nears, the excitement mounts because time is now beginning to put pressure on you. You'll want to check the odds as late as you can before you put your bet together. To do this, you must be already in line if the lines are long, or at least standing near the ticket windows in case long lines begin to form. There are television monitors near the windows that display the same information found on the infield's tote board.

If the odds on a horse you've marked with a green line continue to drop, simply extend the green line accordingly. If the odds on a green-line horse begin to rise, do nothing. It's not unusual for a horse's odds to go down and then rise as the betting eventually rights itself. It's even possible that a horse you marked with a long green line will go to the post at its opening odds. You did your job; you caught the drop in odds; hopefully, your work will pay off.

Now we're ready to fill in the wheel. The two horses you will want on top are (1) the horse with the longest green line (if more than one horse has the same longest lines, choose the horse with the highest odds as of that moment), and (2) the horse with a yellow line with the highest odds as of that moment. These two horses will also be listed in the place and show positions.

The third horse to add to the place and show positions will have the next longest green line. Again, if there is more than one horse with the same length line, choose the horse with the highest odds among them.

The fourth horse to add to the show position will be chosen among the remaining two yellow-lined horses and any green-lined horses that are left. Simply pick the horse with the highest odds. It's possible that you'll be choosing among relatively high odds for this position, and that's fine. It's also likely that you'll have two yellow-lined horses in your wheel, which generally means the price will be relatively low if you hit it. Personally, I'm very comfortable having two yellow-lined horses in my wheel, and find that I sometimes bias my selection process for the 4th pick by not counting any remaining green-lined horses if the lines are really short. I'll let you tweak this aspect of the strategy yourself.

Now you know why it's important that you do not draw the green lines until about halfway through the betting period. If you begin marking the horses too soon, too many might be marked, which would tend to eliminate the two remaining yellow-lined horses from consideration for your show position. Most often, only one, two, or three horses will be green-lined.

When you get to the ticket window to make this bet, here's how you say it: "One-dollar tri, part wheel, 1-2, over the 1-2-3, over the 1-2-3-4." The ticket writer at the window will think you're an experienced handicapper and really know what you're doing. Actually, the ticket writer will find out if you "really know what you're doing" when the time comes to cash the ticket!

The odds of winning the trifecta with a part-wheel bet as I've listed here are hard to pinpoint, but they are probably not as good as you would like to believe. And that doesn't just go for you, it goes for anyone, regardless of the horse selection process used. Tri's are tough. Don't expect to win two or three every night. That's not going to happen. But, over time, I hope the high multiple-odds payouts make up for some dry spells. In *Smart Gambling* vernacular, tri's are a great way to enjoy the "anticipation" of a big win!

You should also know that there are some situations where you won't be able to make the trifecta wager.

For example, it's possible there will not be enough green-lined horses to fill up your wheel. You need at least two. If you can't fill it up, you'll have to pass on the bet. Which reminds me… don't make up your own rules just so you can make the wager. Not a good idea.

One of the reasons you might not be able to mark enough horses with green lines is because the favorites are getting all the money, in which case, the odds on many of the other horses will be rising instead of dropping. Don't hesitate to pass up a race.

In fact, I never bet a trifecta if the favorite is going off at less than even-money. The reason I won't bet is because I would most likely not have that favorite in my wheel. And I don't like going against a horse that looks that good on the tote board. But even if I did have the favorite in my wheel, and the ticket won, the price would probably be so small that it's hardly worth my $8 to go after it.

That's why my selection process always calls for the highest-odds horse available. If you find that betting the highest-odds horses is not working out for you, convert to betting the lowest-odds horses. You should win more often, but the prices will undoubtedly be smaller. I recommend that you add these two clarifications to your strategy.

Another reason you might have to pass on the trifecta is because the track is not offering the bet on that particular race. At the harness tracks, trifectas are offered on nearly all races, but not so at many thoroughbred tracks. Don't ask me why.

For those of you who do not have the patience for bets that win so infrequently, let me suggest an exacta wheel, which is far easier because you only have to pick two horses, not three. But, in line with the reduced odds, you should expect smaller prices.

The Exacta Wheel

We can do the exacta wheel just like the trifecta wheel, but we eliminate a level of selection. Here's how we go after the exacta, looking for the two horses that will finish 1st and 2nd, in exact order.

We're going to pick three horses, total. Two of the horses can either win or place. A third horse can only place. That's it. We have three horses to work with. And, this is even better… our cost for a $1 ticket is only $4. Our ticket is simply a "one-two, over the one-two-three." Here's how our exacta wheel looks on paper:

WIN   1-2
PLACE   1-2-3

To confirm that there are four ways to win:

| 1 | 1 | 2 | 2 |
| 2 | 3 | 1 | 3 |

Here's the way you should think of this bet:
The 1-horse and 2-horse can either win or place.
The 3-horse can place, but it can't win.

Selecting the three horses for the exacta wheel is just like what we did for the trifecta. Mark the favorites with yellow lines. Cross out the long-shots. Wait ten minutes. Get out your green highlighter.

The two horses you will want on top are (1) the horse with the longest green line and (2) the yellow-lined horse sporting the highest odds as of that moment. These two horses will also be listed in the place position.

The third horse to add to the place position will be chosen among the remaining two yellow-lined horses and any green-lined horses that are left. Simply pick the horse with the highest odds.

Natural Progression

Horse racing lends itself to two progressive betting habits that I particularly like. First, you can start with a $1 exacta wheel and "progress" to a $2 wheel if you win. Second, you can start with an exacta wheel and "progress" to a trifecta wheel if you win.

Your starting point each time you visit the track should be a $1 exacta wheel.

Remember that a $1 wheel earns half the payoff. The prices on the tote board are always for a two-dollar ticket. And you should also know that an exacta is more than twice as easy (if *easy* is the right word) as a trifecta.

Starting with a $1 exacta wheel is the smart way to go.

The All-Blaster Strategy

Both the trifecta and exacta part-wheels that we just covered, great bets that they are, still have two minor drawbacks that we should try to resolve, at least for the sake of those of you who are the most tender of all tenderfoots.

For one, you need to know the program picks so you do need a program. A track's program is certainly not as complicated as a racing form, but a little complicated, nonetheless, to a beginner.

Second, you do need to pick either four horses (for your trifecta part-wheel) or three horses (for your exacta part-wheel), so you are, in essence, selecting horses and eliminating horses. True, you're relying on the handicapping of others in making these selections, but the fact remains that certain horses in the race will not be on your ticket. If there are 12 horses in a race, and you're betting an exacta part-wheel, any one of nine horses can make your ticket a useless scrap of paper, just like all the other scraps of paper that get swept off the floor every day.

Remember when we were talking about boxing horses instead of wheeling horses earlier in this chapter? I told you that a great way to ensure a win was to simply box all the horses in a race! Well, the same can be said for a wheel-bet, too. Simply wheel all the horses with all the horses. You would announce the bet by saying: "One-dollar exacta wheel, all over all." A bet like that is no longer a *part*-wheel, it's the *whole* wheel!

Do horse players make bets like that, you ask? Indeed they do. Especially on maiden races (written for young horses, unproven, and yet to find the winner's circle) where the odds can be quite large when no betting favorite emerges. Bets might be distributed rather evenly over the entire field. It's possible that all the horses could be going off at 8 to 1 odds or higher. That's right. It's a perfect time to throw a little luck into your ticket.

Let me give you a perfect example, a freshly brewed story that happened on the morning of the day I'm writing these words.

My nearby track has completed its live racing meet but the doors are still open. The few cars in the parking lot belong to the die-hards who would rather bet Santa Anita or Gulfstream or the Meadowlands, anyhow. Indeed. The track is open for "simulcasting," which means televising another track's races for betting purposes. The signal, say, from Churchill Downs, is transmitted via satellite to tracks all over the country, not to mention race books in Nevada and Atlantic City casinos and other off-track betting parlors.

A ticket writer at my track can push the button for Churchill Downs and out comes a ticket written at the same odds (called "track odds") as if I were in Louisville, Kentucky instead of Muskegon, Michigan.

Virtually all tracks today offer simulcasting, whether the local track has live racing or not. And when it's just simulcasting, it's my favorite time to visit the track. No crowds, no watchers. Just serious players. And a plethora of tracks to choose from.

After I snooped over the shoulders of some of my buddies, asking that classic question that seems more fitting when walking along Muskegon's pier when the salmon are running—"Catch anything?"—I watched a couple of races and then settled in. I was ready to fish out some winners.

My first bet lost; I boxed the 4-5-7, picking the 7 over the 8 in a nail-biter. The 5 won easily, the 4 was a close second, the 8 was a distant third, beating out... you guessed it... the 7 by a nose. The tri paid $377 and I wanted to shoot myself.

The second wager I made was the score. I hit the target so cleanly that I still can't believe how easy it was. I couldn't find the winner but I liked the 7. I liked the 7 a lot, but not enough to put him on top in a part-wheel. It was a maiden race full of long-odds horses that I love to play. As I said earlier, It's where the real money is, if... and this is a big if... you can pick the right horses to fill your box. But I wasn't going to box this race. And even a part-wheel wasn't the answer, either. I can't pick the long shots any better than any-one else. Boxing or part-wheeling three horses, or even four, was the wrong way to bet this race, for I would be only guessing, and hoping, for a big-numbered horse to walk me to the winner's circle.

There's a right way to bet a race that's full of long-shots. Where most handicappers shy away from races of this sort because of the unpredictability, I look for them like a flashing beacon on my radar screen. And then I zero in.

The bet I made is called an "all" ticket. Not all over all, of course. That's too expensive. I made a bet that took advantage of both the "wheel" concept and the "all" concept of betting. Remember, "all" means exactly what it sounds like. It means *all the horses*. Or, in the case of my exacta wheel, it meant all the horses other than my 7.

So where did I put the 7? Remember that I didn't like the 7 to win, so that meant only one thing if I were going to bet this race (and I'm thankful I did): I put the 7 in the place position and *all* the other horses on top. **I like the All-Blaster's strategy of picking the 2nd place horse instead of the winner. By doing so, you're clearly going *with* the odds because the odds say you *won't* pick the winner. And that's fine. You don't have to!**

To determine the cost for a $1 ticket, simply subtract one from the number of horses in the race. A $2 exacta is double that amount. For this race, there were ten horses, so my bet cost $18. (I could have made this bet for one dollar instead of two, but my hunch was too strong to play conservatively.

Cost Of An All-Blaster Ticket

1ST (Win)	2ND (Place)	Horses In Race	COST	
			$1*	$2
ALL	PICK	8	7	14
HORSES	ANY	9	8	16
OTHER	ONE	10	9	18
THAN	HORSE	11	10	20
YOUR		12	11	22
PICK				

*Wins one-half of exacta price (payoff)

Here's how to state this bet to the ticket writer: "One-dollar exacta wheel, all over 7" (using the 7-horse by way of example as your choice for the place position, and one dollar per way as your choice for the amount to wager).

Simply stated, my ticket wins if the 7 comes in second, regardless of who wins. There were five high-odds horses going off because two of the horses were decent favorites at 5 to 2 and 2 to 1. My 7 went to post at 6 to 1. If one of the lower-odds horses had topped the race, my ticket wouldn't have been worth much. But any of the seven other horses would make a nice, early Christmas present. And I had them. I had them all. All I needed was for one of these unproven non-winners to top off my ticket and beat the 7 to the wire.

Maiden races are usually short because the horses are young and inexperienced. They bump and grind their way around the track, learning the techniques that might someday make them a champion. But not today, so you don't throw a mile and a quarter at them. Five furlongs is typical. I would know in quick order whether or not my All-Blaster hit the target.

The gates open and it's a free-for-all, with the horses all bunched up through the backstretch. The two favorites pull out and I'm looking at a worthless ticket. But then my 7 makes a move, and the 3 comes on strong on the outside. Shoot! It looks as if the 7 is going to beat the 30-to-1 long-shot as it pulls away. But it tires in the deep stretch and the 3 goes on to win; my 7 is second… barely, and my ticket is starting to smoke.

I can't wait for the prices to pop up on the screen; all the while the camera is focused on this beautiful filly who just beat the boys in her first win.

She pays a whopping $64.80 to win, my 7 gets a decent $10.80 to place, and the 8, another long-shot, fills out the board at $13.30 to show. I'm thinking the trifecta must be huge, but I'm only interested in the exacta. And they make me wait. Apparently these big prices take longer to light up. All those extra bulbs, right?

Finally! The board flashes the $2 exacta price of $560.00! The tri was an impressive four thousand dollars and change! Someone must have bet an all-7-all, for I know of no other way to handicap a race like this one other than dumb-luck picking.

I cashed that ticket and grabbed my overcoat on the way to the door. That's right. The door. My mission was over and it's back to the base with the biggest exacta I've even captured.

Mission accomplished.

And you can do it, too. If your mission is like mine, learn how to bet "all" tickets. They can be your finest weapon at the racetrack. But be careful. "All-Blaster" tickets are not cheap. You must learn when to use them. Like so many other facets of gambling, it's all a matter of timing.

OK. So now we've resolved one of the problems I spoke of earlier: eliminating horses. But to eliminate using a program takes some guts. Let me take you back to a Las Vegas trip I fondly recall, and the race I bet without even the benefit of a pencil.

I was staying at the Las Vegas Hilton, in town for a bookseller's convention. Every breakfast, lunch, and dinner during a convention is written off as "entertainment" expenses because sellers want to corral the buyers and, well, entertain them. Actually, they want to sell them. Books, in this case. And what better way than to invite three of a top book-chain's buyers to dinner at the Las Vegas Hilton, expecting an enjoyable evening with friends. What I didn't know was that none of them had been to Vegas before. And what I was expecting was different from what they were expecting. They knew all about my books. They knew about my reputation. What they were expecting was a crash course in winning! At every game!

We hit every table game and won! They didn't make their own bets; they bet *my* bets. That's right. Wherever I placed a chip on the roulette table, that's where they put their chips, too. And at the blackjack tables, they simply added their chips to my chips, the same stack, in the same betting circle. They even mimicked every bet I made at the dice tables, too. And why not! We were on one incredible ride!

The race book at the Hilton is impressive. Sports betting and horse-racing and a great little deli and video poker machines scattered all over. My buyer-friends had all walked through it earlier, but had no clue what to do. Well, now they were ready to bring the Hilton to its knees.

We all made a tidy bet on a Saturday morning game, so that took care of the sports-betting aspect of our gambling marathon. Next it was on to the big screens to watch harness racing, and *only* harness racing, because that was all that was available. In those days, thoroughbreds only raced in the afternoons while trotters took over the evenings. A quick scan of the race book's giant screens showed that we had only three tracks to choose from. It would be the toughest test of the night. A quick scan of the race book itself showed nary a soul in sight. Harness racing among Vegas bettors just doesn't draw.

So here were four lonely bettors out West staring at three sloppy tracks out East. I've always said that if a harness track is muddy, you might as well throw darts at the program. But we didn't even have a program!

I told my friends that we'd pick a long-shot horse and put him second in an exacta wheel with all the other horses on top. They didn't know what the hell I was talking about but they were game for anything. It took me a few minutes to pick the track, and the horse, and we were ready to wager. We all chipped in and made the bet for $80. No big deal. After all, our pockets were full of chips.

I won't keep you in suspense. The 2-horse in the last race at the Meadowlands went off at 7 to 1 (bet down from 11 to 1) and fought the favorite all the way around the mile track in an exciting race. He finished exactly where we wanted him. Second. Unfortunately, the strong 3 to 1 favorite won the race, so I explained to my "class" that we should not expect a windfall. But the payoff was better than I expected. We each earned $65 for our $20 investment.

I can tell you where my friends' profits probably ended up. In the gullet of the casino's video poker machines. My profits stayed in my pocket as I wished them good luck... and good night.

Let me tell you exactly how I picked the right horse. Here's a list of the conditions I look for when betting an All-Blaster with *or without* a program:

1. **No odds-on favorites.** A horse going off at even money or better clearly reduces the likelihood of a high exacta payoff.

2. **No more than two horses at 3 to 1 or better.** Three or more horses at 3 to 1 or better would suggest that the race is only among those horses.

3. **At least one horse at 5, 6, or 7 to 1.** My pick will be from this mid-odds group. If there are more than one horse within this range, I'll pick the horse with the higher odds. Track studies have shown that 2nd-place finishers often come from this group.

4. **At least two long-shot horses, at odds of 10 to 1 or higher.** Without the long-shots, there's little hope of a huge win.

5. **No more than 12 horses in the race, and no less than 8 horses.** Smaller fields generally result in smaller prices. Large fields simply make the selection process too difficult.

6. **An off-track.** A distinct *dis*advantage if we're looking for the winning horse as most handicappers are,
but we're not. More important, we need the added
uncertainty to increase the possibility of a long-shot
topping the field.

7. **An allowance (conditioned) race.** Never a claiming or stakes race. Claiming races and especially
stakes races do not produce the frequency of high
exacta prices we're looking for.

All odds quoted are late odds when the horses are
called to the starting gate.

My Personal Advice

As you get more accustomed to handicapping, you
might actually want to do at least some studying to help
you decide if you think the changing odds are correct.
If you do get to the point where you want to review
past performances, let me make clear exactly what
you're looking for: **You are not looking for the horse
that *should* win today. You are looking for the horse
that *will* win today.** And there's a huge difference.

It's no different from the bane of sports bettors:
watching a team lose that should have won; a team far
superior in talent but one that inexplicably falls short
on the scoreboard. A college basketball team, for
example, might have a lackluster regular season, but
come to terms with its potential for winning in the
NCAA tournament. The smart handicapper will know
that this team comes of age in the tournament. The
makings were there: good coaching, teamwork, free-

throw shooting, strong defense, and so on, but the team was rarely inspired during the regular season.

Believe it or not, horses are really no different. Sometimes they feel like racing hard and sometimes they don't. Like humans, they need motivation... a desire to win.

A good handicapper can look deep into a horse's racing performance in the hope of finding a clue that will lend predictability to today's race. Are all the conditions here that will spark that desire to win?

If I were to elaborate on all the points that can help you read the racing form, I might as well write the 535th book on horse racing, but that's not the intent of this chapter. I make mention of this simply so you can see that picking horses by studying past performances is a frustrating, grueling process. Only a few handicappers I know have the stamina and the analytical mind to make it work for them.

For the rest of us, *Smart Gambling* answers a lot of the concerns of new players. It's easy, it's fun, and it's potentially very profitable!

I hope you decide to give horse racing a try. If you are fortunate enough to live near a major track, that's all the better. If you live in Southern California, for example, you can visit my favorite cathedrals of horse racing: Santa Anita and Del Mar. Other states are noted for horse racing, too: Florida, New York, New Jersey, Maryland, Ohio, Illinois, Kentucky, Arkansas, Louisiana, and Texas, for example, have great tracks steeped in rich tradition.

Keep the tradition alive.

Enjoy the sport of kings!